The Sainsbury Book of
SUPPERS
& SNACKS
Caroline Ellwood

CONTENTS

NOTES

Standard spoon measurements are used in all
recipes
1 tablespoon=one 15 ml spoon
1 teaspoon=one 5 ml spoon
All spoon measures are level.

Fresh herbs are used unless otherwise stated. If
unobtainable substitute a bouquet garni of the
equivalent dried herbs, or use dried herbs instead
but halve the quantities stated.

Use freshly ground black pepper where pepper is
specified.

Size 3 eggs should be used unless otherwise stated.

Ovens should be preheated to the specified
temperature.

For all recipes, quantities are given in both metric
and imperial measures. Follow either set but not a
mixture of both, because they are not
interchangeable.

Published exclusively for
J Sainsbury plc
Stamford Street, London SE1 9LL
by Cathay Books
59 Grosvenor Street, London W1

First published 1983

© Cathay Books 1983
ISBN 0 86178 190 2

Printed in Hong Kong

INTRODUCTION

This invaluable series addition provides plenty of exciting new ideas for tasty suppers and snacks. All too frequently these meals are associated with convenience foods, but the recipes in this book are designed to make the most of fresh ingredients.

There are recipes for all kinds of occasions, from tray meals for quiet winter evenings in front of the television, to tasty salads and outdoor picnics to enjoy in warmer weather. For packed lunches, there are delicious, economical alternatives to the traditional cheese or ham sandwiches. No need to panic when friends drop in unexpectedly either – quick and easy special occasion meals are included.

Toasted sandwiches, pizzas and flans are always popular, and a toasted sandwich maker is a useful appliance for speedy snacks. Mixers, blenders and food processors can also cut down preparation time. Those with little time to spend in the kitchen will find plenty of time-saving snacks to choose from in this original cookbook.

TOASTED SANDWICHES, PIZZAS & FLANS

Toasted Cheese Rarebit

25 g (1 oz) butter
1 teaspoon dry
   mustard
250 g (8 oz)
   matured Cheddar
   cheese, grated
3-4 tablespoons pale
   or brown ale
pinch of cayenne
   pepper
1 tablespoon chopped
   chives
salt and pepper
6 slices hot buttered
   toast

Melt the butter in a heavy-based pan, add the mustard and mix until smooth. Stir in the cheese, beer, cayenne, chives, and salt and pepper to taste. Stir over a low heat, until the cheese has melted and the mixture is creamy.

Spoon over the toast and cook under a preheated hot grill for 1 to 2 minutes, until golden brown and bubbling. Serve immediately.
Serves 6

Tomato and Cheese Toasted Open Sandwich

4 slices brown bread
butter for spreading
4 large tomatoes,
    skinned and
    thickly sliced
salt and pepper
4 basil sprigs,
    roughly chopped
75 g (3 oz) matured
    Cheddar cheese,
    grated
4 rashers bacon,
    derinded and
    halved

Toast the bread on both sides and spread one side with butter. Arrange the tomatoes on the buttered side and season with salt and pepper to taste. Sprinkle with the basil and cheese, and top with 2 bacon pieces.

Cook under a preheated hot grill for 5 to 7 minutes, until the bacon is cooked and the cheese bubbling. Serve immediately.

Serves 4

Italian Fried Sandwiches

2 teaspoons made
   mustard
8 slices buttered
   white bread, crusts
   removed
125 g (4 oz)
   Gruyère cheese,
   sliced
2 eggs
1 tablespoon oil
salt and pepper
oil for shallow-frying

Spread the mustard evenly over the buttered side of the bread. Arrange the cheese on 4 slices and top with the remaining bread.

Beat the eggs and oil together, adding salt and pepper to taste. Dip each sandwich into this mixture.

Heat the oil in a frying pan and fry 2 sandwiches at a time until golden brown; drain on kitchen paper. Serve immediately.

Serves 4

Prawn and Cheese Toasties

For this recipe use a special toasted sandwich maker.

175 g (6 oz) frozen
   peeled prawns,
   thawed and
   chopped
2 eggs, hard-boiled
   and chopped
125 g (4 oz) double
   Gloucester cheese
   with chives, grated
salt and pepper
8 slices buttered bread
1-2 teaspoons sesame
   seeds

Mix the prawns, eggs and cheese, seasoning well with salt and pepper. Sprinkle the buttered side of the bread with the sesame seeds, pressing them evenly over the surface; shake off any excess.

Place 4 slices, buttered side down, in the preheated sandwich toaster. Spread with the prawn mixture and cover with the remaining bread, butter side up. Lower the lid and toast for 2 to 3 minutes, or according to maker's instructions. Serve hot.

Serves 4

Croque Monsieur

8 slices Gruyère
   cheese
4 slices ham
8 slices white bread,
   buttered
1 egg, beaten
fresh breadcrumbs for
   coating
oil for shallow-frying

Arrange the cheese and ham slices alternately on 4 slices of bread. Top with the remaining bread, pressing the sandwich together. Coat with beaten egg and breadcrumbs.

Heat the oil in a frying pan and fry 2 sandwiches at a time until golden brown; drain on kitchen paper. Cut in half and serve immediately.

Serves 4

Prawn and Tuna Pizzette

½ teaspoon dried
  yeast
½ teaspoon caster
  sugar
175 g (6 oz) strong
  white plain flour
pinch of salt
50 g (2 oz) butter
1 egg, beaten
little milk to mix
FILLING:
1 × 64 g (2¼ oz)
  can tomato purée
250 g (8 oz)
  tomatoes, skinned
1 × 99 g (3½ oz)
  can tuna, drained
50 g (2 oz) peeled
  prawns
½ teaspoon each dried
  oregano and basil
1 tablespoon olive oil
50 g (2 oz) Bel Paese
  cheese, cubed
few black olives
1 × 50 g (1¾ oz)
  can anchovy fillets

Dissolve the yeast and sugar in a little warm water. Sift the flour and salt into a bowl and rub in the butter until the mixture resembles fine breadcrumbs. Mix in the egg, dissolved yeast and a little milk to give a firm dough. Knead for 5 to 10 minutes, until the dough is smooth and elastic. Place in a bowl, cover with a cloth and leave to rise in a warm place for 1½ hours or until doubled in size.

Knead again, divide into 8 pieces and roll out into circles. Place on baking sheets and spread with the tomato purée. Slice the tomatoes and arrange on top. Cover with the tuna and prawns. Sprinkle with the herbs and a little olive oil. Bake in a preheated moderately hot oven, 200°C (400°F), Gas Mark 6, for 10 minutes.

Top with the cheese, olives and anchovy fillets. Return to the oven for 5 minutes. Serve hot or cold.
Serves 4 to 8

Pan Pizza

½ teaspoon dried yeast
½ teaspoon caster
  sugar
75 g (3 oz) strong
  white plain flour
75 g (3 oz)
  wholemeal flour
pinch of salt
50 g (2 oz) butter
1 egg, beaten
little milk to mix
FILLING:
1 × 64 g (2¼ oz)
  can tomato purée
250 g (8 oz) tomatoes,
  skinned and sliced
1 clove garlic, sliced
½ teaspoon each dried
  oregano and basil
75 g (3 oz) Bel Paese
  cheese, cubed
1 × 340 g (12 oz) can
  asparagus, drained
125 g (4 oz) tiny
  button mushrooms
few stuffed olives

Dissolve the yeast and sugar in a little warm water. Place the flours and salt in a bowl and rub in the butter until the mixture resembles fine bread-crumbs. Mix in the egg, dissolved yeast and a little milk to give a firm dough. Knead for 5 to 10 minutes, until smooth and elastic. Place in a bowl, cover with a cloth and leave to rise in a warm place for 1½ hours, until doubled in size.

Lightly grease a large heavy-based frying pan. Knead the dough again and roll out on a floured surface to the pan size. Place in the pan and bring a little dough up the sides.

Spread the tomato purée over the base, arrange the tomatoes on top and sprinkle with the garlic, herbs and cheese. Arrange the asparagus, mushrooms and olives on top.

Cook over a medium heat for 15 to 20 minutes, then place under a preheated hot grill for 1 to 2 minutes, until the cheese is golden. Serve hot.
Serves 4 to 6

Baby Pizzas

1 quantity pizza
 dough (see method)
1 quantity tomato
 sauce (see method)
TOPPING:
125 g (4 oz)
 Mozzarella
 cheese, diced
1 tablespoon grated
 Parmesan cheese
125 g (4 oz) Italian
 Mortadella or
 salami, chopped
1-2 cloves garlic,
 crushed

Prepare the pizza dough and tomato
sauce as for Pizza Napoletana
(below). When the dough has risen,
knead it again and divide into 8 or
12 pieces. Form each into a round.

Heat a little oil in a large frying
pan and fry 2 or 3 rounds at a time
for about 5 to 7 minutes, until
golden brown on each side.

Spread the hot sauce on the pizzas
and top with the cheeses, Mortadella
or salami and garlic. Return to the
pan and cook for 3 minutes. Fold in
half and serve immediately.
Serves 4 to 6

Pizza Napoletana

PIZZA DOUGH:
300 g (10 oz) strong
 white plain flour
pinch of salt
1 teaspoon dried yeast
1 teaspoon caster
 sugar
250 ml (8 fl oz) warm
 water (approx)
TOMATO SAUCE:
1 tablespoon oil
1 onion, chopped
1 clove garlic, crushed
1 × 397 g (14 oz)
 can tomatoes
2 tablespoons dry
 white wine
1/2 teaspoon each dried
 oregano and basil
salt and pepper
1 tablespoon tomato
 purée
TOPPING:
125 g (4 oz) Mozza-
 rella or Cheddar
 cheese, diced
1 tablespoon capers
 (optional)

Sift the flour and salt into a bowl.
Mix the yeast with the sugar and
2 tablespoons of the water and leave
for 10 minutes, then add to the flour
with enough water to give a firm
dough. Knead on a floured surface for
about 15 minutes, until the dough is
elastic. Cover with a cloth and leave
in a warm place until doubled in size.

Press the dough into the base and
sides of a 23 cm (9 inch) loose-
bottomed tin or flan ring placed on a
baking sheet.

Heat the oil in a pan, add the
onion and garlic and cook for 2 to
3 minutes, until translucent. Add the
tomatoes with their juice, the wine,
herbs, and salt and pepper to taste.
Bring to the boil and cook rapidly
for 12 to 15 minutes, until thickened.
Stir in the tomato purée.

Spread evenly over the dough and
arrange the cheese and capers, if
using, on top. Bake in a preheated
hot oven, 220°C (425°F), Gas Mark 7,
for 20 minutes, until golden brown.

Serve hot.
Serves 6 to 8

Rustica Pie

PASTRY:

250 g (8 oz) plain
   flour
pinch of salt
175 g (6 oz) butter
squeeze of lemon
   juice
little iced water to
   mix

FILLING:

3 eggs, beaten
350 g (12 oz)
   Ricotta or cottage
   cheese
125 g (4 oz)
   Parmesan cheese,
   grated
1 onion, chopped
2 tablespoons
   chopped chives
salt and pepper
1 tablespoon oil
2 cloves garlic, crushed
350 g (12 oz)
   tomatoes, skinned,
   seeded and chopped
1 × 64 g (2¼ oz)
   can tomato purée
4 tablespoons dry
   white wine
½ teaspoon each
   dried marjoram
   and oregano
125 g (4 oz) black
   olives, stoned
250 g (8 oz)
   Mozzarella
   cheese, sliced
1 green pepper,
   seeded, cored and
   thinly sliced

Sift the flour and salt into a bowl and rub in the butter until the mixture resembles fine breadcrumbs. Add the lemon juice and enough water to give a firm dough. Cover and chill for 30 minutes.

Meanwhile, prepare the filling. Mix together the eggs, cheeses, onion and chives. Season well with salt and pepper.

Heat the oil in a pan, add the garlic and cook for 1 minute, without browning. Stir in the tomatoes, tomato purée, wine, herbs and salt and pepper to taste. Bring to the boil and cook rapidly for about 15 minutes, until thickened; cool.

Divide the pastry in half. Roll out one piece and use to line a 23 cm (9 inch) pie dish. Roll out the other piece for a lid.

Spread half the cheese mixture over the base. Sprinkle over half the olives and arrange half the cheese slices on top. Spoon over half the tomato sauce and arrange half the pepper slices on top. Repeat the layers and cover with the pastry lid. Seal and flute the edges and make 3 or 4 diagonal slashes through the lid.

Bake in a preheated hot oven, 220°C (425°F), Gas Mark 7, for 35 minutes, until golden brown.

Leave for 30 minutes before serving.

Serves 6 to 8

French Bread Pizzas

1 French loaf
BASE:
1 × 64 g (2¼ oz)
  can tomato purée
1-2 teaspoons dried
  mixed herbs
1-2 cloves garlic,
  crushed (optional)

TOPPING:
4 tomatoes, sliced
125 g (4 oz) salami
8 rashers streaky
  bacon, derinded
2 tablespoons capers
125 g (4 oz) Gruyère
  cheese, grated

Cut the bread in half lengthways and spread the tomato purée over the cut surfaces. Sprinkle with the herbs and garlic, if using.

Arrange the sliced tomatoes and salami on each piece of French bread. Lay the bacon on top, sprinkle with the capers and top with the cheese.

Cut each piece of bread into four. Place on lightly oiled baking sheets and bake in a preheated moderately hot oven, 200°C (400°F), Gas Mark 6, for 15 minutes. Serve hot.

Serves 4 to 8

NOTE: Topping ingredients can be varied according to taste.

Quiche Provençal

250 g (8 oz) plain
  flour
pinch of salt
75 g (3 oz) butter
25 g (1 oz) lard
1 egg yolk
iced water to mix
FILLING:
25 g (1 oz) butter
1 onion, sliced
1 clove garlic, crushed
50 g (2 oz) button
  mushrooms, sliced
1 courgette, chopped
2 large tomatoes,
  skinned and chopped
few basil leaves,
  chopped
½ teaspoon dried
  mixed herbs
salt and pepper
2 eggs
142 ml (5 fl oz)
  single cream
50 g (2 oz) Cheddar
  cheese, grated
25 g (1 oz) Gruyère
  cheese, sliced

Sift the flour and salt into a bowl and rub in the fats until the mixture looks like fine breadcrumbs. Stir in the egg yolk and enough water to make a firm dough. Turn onto a floured surface and knead lightly. Roll out and use to line a 23 cm (9 inch) flan ring placed on a baking sheet. Prick all over and chill for 30 minutes.

Line with foil and dried beans and bake 'blind' in a preheated moderately hot oven, 190°C (375°F), Gas Mark 5, for 12 to 15 minutes, until set. Remove the foil and beans and return to the oven for 5 minutes.

Melt the butter in a pan, add the onion and garlic and cook gently for 5 minutes. Add the vegetables and herbs and season well with salt and pepper. Cook for 10 minutes.

Beat the eggs and cream together and stir in the grated cheese.

Spoon the tomato mixture into the flan case, pour over the egg mixture and carefully arrange the cheese slices on top. Bake for 25 to 30 minutes, until set. Serve hot or cold.
Serves 6 to 8

Quiche Paysanne

75 g (3 oz) plain
  flour, sifted
75 g (3 oz)
  wholemeal flour
pinch of salt
75 g (3 oz) margarine
4-5 tablespoons iced
  water
FILLING:
15 g (½ oz) butter
1 tablespoon oil
4 rashers bacon,
  derinded and
  chopped
1 large onion, chopped
2 potatoes, sliced
2 eggs
142 ml (5 fl oz)
  double cream
1 tablespoon each
  chopped parsley
  and chives
salt and pepper
½ red pepper, cored,
  seeded and
  chopped (optional)
75 g (3 oz) Cheddar
  cheese, grated

Place the flours and salt in a bowl
and rub in the margarine until the
mixture resembles fine breadcrumbs.
Add enough water to make a firm
dough. Turn onto a floured surface
and knead lightly. Roll out and use
to line a 20 cm (8 inch) flan ring on a
baking sheet. Prick all over and chill
for 30 minutes. Bake blind as for
Quiche Provençal (opposite).

Heat the butter and oil in a pan,
add the bacon and cook until lightly
browned. Drain on kitchen paper.
Add the onion and potatoes to the pan
and cook for 12 to 15 minutes, until
browned. Drain on kitchen paper.

Beat the eggs and cream together,
stir in the herbs and season well with
salt and pepper.

Spoon the potatoes, onion and
bacon into the flan case and sprinkle
over the red pepper, if using. Pour
over the egg mixture and sprinkle
with the cheese. Return to the oven
for 20 to 25 minutes, until well risen
and golden brown. Serve hot or cold.
Serves 4 to 6

Watercress and Onion Flan

75 g (3 oz) plain
  flour, sifted
75 g (3 oz)
  wholemeal flour
pinch of salt
40 g (1½ oz)
  margarine
40 g (1½ oz) lard
2 tablespoons grated
  Parmesan cheese
1 egg yolk
iced water to mix
FILLING:
25 g (1 oz) butter
1 bunch spring
  onions, chopped
1 bunch watercress,
  finely chopped
3 eggs
142 ml (5 fl oz)
  soured cream
125 g (4 oz) Cheddar
  cheese, grated
TO GARNISH:
watercress sprigs

Place the flours and salt in a bowl and rub in the fats until the mixture resembles fine breadcrumbs. Stir in the Parmesan and egg yolk and add a little water to make a firm dough. Turn onto a floured surface and knead lightly. Roll out and use to line a 20 cm (8 inch) flan ring placed on a baking sheet. Prick all over and chill for 30 minutes. Bake blind as for Quiche Provençal (page 16).

Melt the butter in a pan, add the onions and cook, without browning, for 5 minutes. Stir in the watercress and cook for 2 minutes, until soft.

Beat the eggs and soured cream together, stir in the cheese and season well with salt and pepper.

Spoon the onion and watercress into the flan case. Pour over the egg mixture and return to the oven for 20 to 25 minutes, until golden brown.

Serve hot or cold, garnished with watercress.

Serves 4 to 6

Prawn Cheesecake

125 g (4 oz) butter
250 g (8 oz) Cheddar
  cheese biscuits
4 tablespoons grated
  Parmesan cheese
113 g (4 oz) cream
  cheese
1 teaspoon French
  mustard
125 g (4 oz) Gruyère
  cheese, grated
3 eggs, beaten
142 ml (5 fl oz)
  soured cream
250 g (8 oz) peeled
  prawns, chopped
1 tablespoon each
  chopped parsley
  and chives
4 spring onions,
  chopped
TO GARNISH:
whole cooked prawns
thyme or parsley
  sprigs

Melt the butter and crush the biscuits. Combine the butter, biscuit crumbs and 2 tablespoons of the Parmesan cheese. Press onto the base and sides of a 20 cm (8 inch) loose-bottomed flan tin. Chill for 1 hour.

Beat the cream cheese until soft, then stir in the mustard, Gruyère cheese and remaining Parmesan. Gradually stir in the eggs. Fold in the soured cream, prawns, herbs and spring onions.

Spoon the mixture into the prepared flan case and bake in a preheated moderate oven, 180°C (350°F), Gas Mark 4, for 40 to 45 minutes, until golden brown.

Garnish with prawns and sprigs of herbs. Serve cold with a salad.

Serves 6

TRAY MEALS

Orange–Glazed Ham

6 gammon steaks,
   about 5 mm
   (¼ inch) thick
GLAZE:
2 teaspoons French
   mustard
150 ml (¼ pint)
   orange juice
2 tablespoons soft
   brown sugar
grated rind of
   1 orange
½ teaspoon ground
   cloves

TO GARNISH:
1 orange, sliced
thyme sprigs
   (optional)

Put the glaze ingredients in a pan, bring slowly to the boil, then simmer for 5 minutes. Leave to cool, then spread over both sides of the gammon steaks. If possible, leave to marinate for 20 to 30 minutes.

Place under a preheated moderate grill and cook for 5 to 7 minutes on each side, basting occasionally with the remaining glaze.

Transfer to serving plates, spoon over the pan juices and garnish with orange slices, and thyme if liked.
Serves 6

Skewered Chicken with Sage

6 large boneless
   chicken breasts
1 teaspoon French
   mustard
4 tablespoons olive
   oil
2 tablespoons lemon
   or lime juice
1 clove garlic, sliced
1 teaspoon dried
   mixed herbs
salt and pepper
6 rashers streaky
   bacon, derinded
   and halved
few sage sprigs
TO GARNISH:
lemon or lime slices
sage leaves

Cut the chicken into 4 cm (1½ inch)
cubes. Put the mustard, oil, lemon or
lime juice and garlic in a bowl and
mix well. Stir in the herbs, and
season with salt and pepper to taste.
Add the chicken, stir well and leave
to marinate for 20 to 30 minutes.

Roll up the bacon pieces. Thread
the chicken and bacon alternately on
6 skewers, interspersing with sage
leaves to taste. Cook under a
preheated hot grill for 5 to 7 minutes
on each side, until golden and tender;
spoon over the marinade during
cooking.

Garnish with lemon or lime slices
and sage and serve immediately,
with buttered noodles, green salad or
vegetables.
Serves 6

Indian Kebab

750 g (1½ lb)
  minced beef
1 small onion, grated
2 cloves garlic,
  crushed
1 tablespoon tomato
  purée
juice of ½ lemon or
  1 lime
1 tablespoon plain
  flour
½ teaspoon each
  ground cumin,
  chilli powder and
  coriander
pinch each of ground
  cinnamon, ginger,
  nutmeg and cloves
salt and pepper
TO GARNISH:
few lettuce leaves,
  shredded
lemon twists
cucumber slices
mint sprigs

Put the meat, onion, garlic, tomato purée, lemon or lime juice and flour in a bowl and mix well. Stir in all the spices and mix thoroughly. Season well with salt and pepper and mix until smooth.

Divide the mixture into 6 portions and shape around skewers to make long thin rissoles. Refrigerate if possible for 1 to 2 hours until firm.

Place under a preheated hot grill and cook for 15 to 20 minutes, turning occasionally, until well browned.

Arrange the kebabs on a bed of lettuce, garnish with lemon twists, cucumber slices and mint, and serve hot, with rice.
Serves 6

Chilli Chicken Livers

1 tablespoon oil
1 large onion, thinly
   sliced
2 cloves garlic,
   crushed
1 × 397 g (14 oz)
   can tomatoes
1 tablespoon tomato
   purée
1 teaspoon dried
   mixed herbs
1-2 teaspoons chilli
   powder
1 chilli, seeded and
   roughly chopped
salt and pepper
350 g (12 oz)
   chicken livers,
   roughly chopped
1 tablespoon plain
   flour
25 g (1 oz) butter
125 g (4 oz) button
   mushrooms, sliced
150 ml (¼ pint) dry
   white wine

Heat the oil in a pan, add the onion
and garlic and cook for 5 minutes,
until transparent but not browned.
Stir in the tomatoes with their juice.
Bring to the boil and cook rapidly
for 5 minutes. Stir in the tomato
purée, herbs, chilli powder, chilli,
and salt and pepper to taste. Bring
back to the boil and cook,
uncovered, for 20 minutes.

Coat the chicken livers with the
flour. Melt the butter in a pan, add
the chicken livers and fry for
5 minutes, until lightly browned.
Drain them on kitchen paper, then
add to the tomato sauce with the
mushrooms and wine. Bring to the
boil and boil rapidly for 5 to 7
minutes.

Check the seasoning and serve
with noodles or rice.
Serves 4 to 6

Spanish Eggs

4 tablespoons oil
2 slices stale bread,
    cubed
2 large potatoes,
    diced
1 onion, chopped
125 g (4 oz) bacon,
    derinded and
    chopped
50 g (2 oz) French
    beans, cut into 5 cm
    (2 inch) lengths
6 tomatoes, skinned,
    seeded and chopped
2 courgettes, thinly
    sliced
8 thin slices garlic
    sausage, diced
4 eggs
1 tablespoon chopped
    parsley to garnish

Heat the oil in a large frying pan, add the bread cubes and fry until browned. Remove and drain on kitchen paper.

Add the potatoes to the pan, toss in the oil and cook for 15 minutes, until browned on all sides. Add the onion and bacon and cook for 2 minutes. Stir in the beans, tomatoes and courgettes and cook for 5 to 7 minutes. Stir in the garlic sausage.

Transfer to a large shallow ovenproof dish and make 4 hollows in the mixture with the back of a spoon; break an egg into each. Bake in a preheated moderate oven, 180°C (350°F), Gas Mark 4, for 12 minutes. Sprinkle over the fried bread and return to the oven for 3 minutes.

Sprinkle with the parsley and serve immediately.
Serves 4

Chicken and Bean Soup

125 g (4 oz)
  flageolet beans
2 leeks
4 celery sticks
2 large onions
1 clove garlic
2 large chicken
  portions
900 ml (1½ pints)
  water
300 ml (½ pint) dry
  cider
salt and pepper
4 tablespoons single
  cream
2 tablespoons each
  chopped dill and
  chives
dill sprigs to garnish
GARLIC BREAD:
1 French stick
80 g (3 oz) Boursin
  with garlic cheese
1 tablespoon each
  chopped chives and
  parsley

Soak the beans overnight in cold water; drain. Chop the leeks and celery; slice the onions and garlic.

Put the chicken portions, water, cider, fresh vegetables and garlic in a large pan. Cover and bring to the boil, then simmer for 35 to 40 minutes, until the chicken is tender.

Remove the chicken from the pan, dice the flesh, cover and set aside. Add the beans to the pan, and cook for 1 hour, until tender.

Transfer to a blender or food processor and work until smooth. Return to the pan and season well with salt and pepper. Add the diced chicken, bring to the boil and cook for 2 to 3 minutes. Stir in the cream and herbs. Garnish with dill and serve with hot garlic bread.

Serves 4 to 6

Garlic Bread: Split the French loaf. Mix the cheese and herbs together and spread over the cut surfaces. Sandwich together, wrap tightly in foil and cook in a preheated moderately hot oven, 200°C (400°F), Gas Mark 6, for 15 to 20 minutes.

Creamed Mushrooms on Toast

50 g (2 oz) butter
1 small onion,
  chopped
350 g (12 oz) small
  button mushrooms
2 tablespoons plain
  flour
300 ml (½ pint) milk
dash of Worcester-
  shire sauce
2 tablespoons single
  cream (optional)
salt and pepper
juice of ½ lemon
4 slices hot buttered
  toast
parsley sprigs to
  garnish

Melt the butter in a pan, add the onion and cook for 5 to 7 minutes, without browning, until tender. Stir in the mushrooms and cook for 1 minute, stirring well. Sprinkle over the flour and mix well. Gradually add the milk, stirring constantly. Bring to the boil, then simmer for 2 minutes. Add the Worcestershire sauce, cream, if using, and salt and pepper to taste. Remove from the heat and stir in the lemon juice.

Put the toast on 4 warmed individual plates and spoon the mushrooms on top. Garnish with parsley and serve immediately.
Serves 4

Asparagus and Cheese Soufflé Omelet

6 eggs, separated
salt and pepper
375 g (12 oz) frozen
  and thawed, or
  canned asparagus
  spears, drained
2 tablespoons water
125 g (4 oz)
  matured Cheddar
  cheese, grated
25 g (1 oz) butter

Put 3 egg yolks in a small bowl with salt and pepper to taste. Reserve a few asparagus spears for garnish; roughly chop the remainder. Stir 1 tablespoon of the water and half the cheese and asparagus into the egg yolks. Whisk the 3 whites until very stiff, then carefully fold into the egg yolk mixture.

Melt half the butter in a 20 cm (8 inch) omelet pan, pour in the egg mixture and spread evenly. Cook over a low heat for 5 minutes, until the underneath is golden brown. Place the pan under a preheated hot grill for 1 minute, until the omelet is lightly browned on top and puffy.

Repeat with the remaining ingredients to make another omelet. Garnish with the reserved asparagus and serve immediately, folded if liked, with garlic bread (see page 25).
Serves 4

Sweetcorn Fritters with Bacon

*2 tablespoons plain
 flour*
*pinch each of salt,
 pepper and
 cayenne*
1 egg, separated
*1 × 326 g (11½ oz)
 can sweetcorn*
oil for shallow-frying
8 rashers bacon

Put the flour and seasonings in a
bowl and mix in the egg yolk. Add
the liquid from the sweetcorn and
mix to a smooth paste, then fold in
the sweetcorn. Whisk the egg white
until stiff and fold into the batter.
Heat the oil in a frying pan. Drop in
spoonfuls of the mixture and brown
on one side, then carefully turn over
to brown the other side. Drain on
kitchen paper and keep hot.

Fry or grill the bacon and serve
immediately, with the fritters.
Serves 4

27

Quick Paella

4 small squid
50 g (2 oz) streaky
   bacon, derinded
125 g (4 oz) chorizo
   or garlic sausage
2 tablespoons oil
3 cloves garlic, sliced
250 g (8 oz)
   long-grain rice
4 tomatoes, skinned,
   seeded and chopped
150 ml (¼ pint) dry
   white wine
150 ml (¼ pint)
   chicken stock
salt and pepper
1 red pepper, cored,
   seeded and chopped
few saffron strands
1 × 397 g (14 oz)
   can artichokes
12 mussels (see note)
125 g (4 oz) peeled
   prawns
lemon slices to
   garnish

Remove the head and ink sac from the squid. Slice the flesh and keep on one side. Dice the bacon and slice the sausage.

Heat the oil in a large frying pan, add the garlic and cook, without browning. Add the bacon and cook for 5 minutes.

Add the rice, tomatoes, wine, stock, and salt and pepper to taste. Bring to the boil, simmer for 5 minutes, then add the red pepper, sausage, saffron and squid. Cook for 10 to 12 minutes, until the rice is tender.

Drain the artichokes and cut into quarters. Add to the pan with the mussels and prawns and cook for 5 minutes.

Garnish with the lemon slices and serve immediately.

Serves 4 to 6

NOTE: Either cooked, shelled fresh mussels or canned ones can be used.

Italian Risotto with Prawns

4 dried cêpes, or 50 g
    (2 oz) flat open
    mushrooms
2 cloves garlic
1 large onion
1 tablespoon oil
15 g (½ oz) butter
175 g (6 oz) Italian or
    short-grain rice
juice of ½ lemon
good pinch of
    chopped thyme
1 tablespoon chopped
    parsley
salt and pepper
300 ml (½ pint) dry
    white wine
300 ml (½ pint) fish
    or chicken stock
1 tablespoon tomato
    purée
250 g (8 oz) peeled
    prawns
4 cooked whole
    prawns to garnish

Soak the cêpes, if using, in warm
water for 15 minutes; squeeze dry.
Slice the cêpes or mushrooms.

Slice the garlic thinly and chop the
onion finely. Heat the oil and butter
in a pan, add the garlic and onion
and sauté until browned. Add the
cêpes or mushrooms, stir in the rice
and cook for 1 minute.

Add the lemon juice, herbs and
salt and pepper to taste; mix well.
Pour over the wine and stock. Bring
to the boil and cook, uncovered, for
12 to 15 minutes, until the rice is
firm but not over-cooked.

Stir in the tomato purée and
increase the heat to reduce any excess
liquid. Stir in the prawns. Garnish
with whole prawns and serve
immediately.
Serves 4

Fettuccine in Four Cheeses

500 g (1 lb) fettuccine
  or tagliatelle
good pinch of salt
2 tablespoons oil
1 onion
2 cloves garlic
SAUCE:
25 g (1 oz) butter
2 cloves garlic, sliced
50 g (2 oz) each
  Emmental, Bel
  Paese, Parmesan
  and Cheddar
  cheese, grated
175 ml (6 fl oz)
  single cream
salt and pepper
TO GARNISH:
1 tablespoon each
  chopped parsley
  and basil

Place the pasta, salt, oil, onion and garlic in a large pan of boiling water and cook for 8 to 9 minutes, until the pasta is just cooked.

Meanwhile, make the sauce. Melt the butter in a pan, add the garlic and cook, without browning, for 3 minutes. Stir in the cheeses and cream and continue stirring over a low heat until the cheeses have melted. Season with salt and pepper to taste.

Drain the pasta and remove the onion and garlic. Toss the pasta in the sauce, sprinkle with the herbs and serve immediately, with a tomato and onion salad.
Serves 4

Pasta Mediterranean

1 tablespoon oil
2 cloves garlic, sliced
1 onion, sliced
1 × 539 g (1 lb 3 oz)
  can tomatoes
150 ml (¼ pint) dry
  white wine
1 teaspoon oregano
1 teaspoon basil
1 tablespoon tomato
  purée
salt and pepper
500 g (1 lb) long
  macaroni
2 teaspoons salt
2 tablespoons oil
175 g (6 oz) peeled
  prawns
125 g (4 oz) shelled
  mussels (see note)
2 tablespoons
  chopped parsley

Heat the oil in a pan, add the garlic and onion and cook for 5 minutes, without browning. Add the tomatoes with their juice, the wine, herbs, tomato purée and salt and pepper to taste. Bring to the boil and cook, uncovered, for 20 to 25 minutes, until thickened.

Meanwhile, break the macaroni into 5 cm (2 inch) lengths. Place in a large pan of boiling water with the salt and oil and cook for 9 to 11 minutes, until just tender.

Add the prawns and mussels to the sauce and cook gently for 5 minutes.

Drain the pasta and arrange on a warmed serving dish. Spoon the sauce over, sprinkle with the parsley and serve immediately.
Serves 4
NOTE: Either cooked, shelled fresh mussels or canned ones can be used.

Jacket Potatoes

Cheap but delicious, these make an excellent accompaniment to grilled meat or, with a tasty filling, an ideal snack on their own.

4 large potatoes
oil for brushing
butter to serve

Brush the potatoes all over with oil and cook in a preheated moderately hot oven, 200°C (400°F), Gas Mark 6, for about 1 hour or until soft.

Cut a large deep cross in one side, fill generously with butter and serve immediately, or use any of the following fillings.

Serves 4

CHIVES AND SOURED CREAM FILLING:

2 egg yolks
142 ml (5 fl oz)
*   soured cream*
dash of Tabasco sauce
2 tablespoons
*   chopped chives*
salt and pepper
spring onions to
*   garnish*

Remove the baked potatoes from the oven, cut in half lengthways, scoop out the flesh and mash until smooth. Beat in the filling ingredients, adding salt and pepper to taste. Spoon the mixture back into the potato shells. Place on a baking sheet and return to the oven for 15 to 20 minutes, until hot and golden brown.

Garnish with spring onions and serve immediately.

Serves 4

BACON AND SALAMI FILLING:

50 g (2 oz) butter
1 large onion, finely
*   chopped*
4 rashers streaky
*   bacon, derinded*
*   and diced*
salt and pepper
25 g (1 oz) salami,
*   diced*
1 tablespoon chopped
*   parsley*
25 g (1 oz) grated
*   Parmesan cheese*
mustard and cress to
*   garnish*

Remove the baked potatoes from the oven, cut in half lengthways, scoop out the flesh and mash until smooth.

Melt the butter in a pan, add the onion and cook until golden brown. Add the bacon and cook for 2 minutes, then stir into the mashed potato. Season well with salt and pepper, stir in the salami and parsley and mix well.

Spoon the mixture back into the potato shells and sprinkle with the cheese. Bake as above.

Garnish with mustard and cress and serve immediately.

Serves 4

SOUFFLÉ CHEESE FILLING:

2 eggs, separated
125 g (4 oz)
  matured Cheddar
  cheese, grated
1 teaspoon English
  mustard
salt and pepper
1 tablespoon grated
  Parmesan cheese
rosemary or parsley
  sprigs to garnish

Remove the baked potatoes from the oven, cut in half lengthways, scoop out the flesh and mash until smooth. Beat in the egg yolks, Cheddar cheese, mustard and salt and pepper to taste.

Whisk the egg whites until very stiff and fold into the mixture. Spoon into the potato shells, sprinkle with the Parmesan and bake as opposite.

Garnish with rosemary or parsley and serve immediately.
Serves 4

SALADS

Fish with Green Mayonnaise

500 g (1 lb) cod fillets
150 ml (¼ pint) dry
  white wine
1 bouquet garni
salt and pepper
250 g (8 oz) peeled
  prawns
250 g (8 oz) spinach
1 clove garlic
  (optional)
4 spring onions
1 tablespoon oil
1 tablespoon lemon
  juice
6 tablespoons
  mayonnaise
4 tablespoons double
  cream

TO GARNISH:
mustard and cress
lemon slices
cooked whole prawns

Place the cod in a shallow frying pan, pour over the wine, add the bouquet garni, and season well with salt and pepper. Bring to the boil and simmer for 7 to 10 minutes, until cooked. Drain and flake the fish. Mix with the prawns.

Place the spinach, garlic, if using, and spring onions in a blender or food processor and work until smooth. Add the oil, lemon juice, mayonnaise and cream and blend again. The mixture should be like thick mayonnaise; if it is too thick add a little more cream or lemon juice to taste. Fold in the fish.

Transfer to individual serving dishes and sprinkle with the mustard and cress. Garnish with lemon slices and prawns to serve.

Serves 4

Kidney Bean Salad

1 × 425 g (15 oz) can
    red kidney beans
1 × 425 g (15 oz) can
    cannellini beans
1 × 397 g (14 oz) can
    artichokes, drained
4 spring onions
2 celery sticks
1 small green pepper,
    cored and seeded
2 eggs, hard-boiled
DRESSING:
1 clove garlic, crushed
120 ml (4 fl oz)
    mayonnaise
1 tablespoon each
    chopped parsley,
    basil and thyme
squeeze of lemon
    juice
salt and pepper
1 tablespoon capers
    (optional)
TO GARNISH:
125 g (4 oz) streaky
    bacon, derinded

Turn the beans into a colander, drain and rinse under cold water; leave to drain thoroughly. Cut the artichokes into quarters.

Place the beans and artichokes in a salad bowl. Chop the spring onions, celery and green pepper and add to the bowl. Cut the eggs into quarters and arrange around the edge.

To make the dressing, mix the garlic, mayonnaise, herbs and lemon juice together. Season well with salt and pepper and stir in the capers, if using. Spoon over the salad and toss well.

Cook the bacon under a preheated hot grill until crisp. Crumble and sprinkle over the salad. Serve immediately.

Serves 4

Rose Salad

½ curly endive or
   2 radicchio
2 × 177 g (6 oz)
   cans crabmeat,
   drained and flaked
150 g (5 oz) peeled
   prawns
juice of ½ lemon
125 g (4 oz) tomatoes
DRESSING:
150 ml (¼ pint)
   mayonnaise
2 teaspoons tomato
   purée
1 clove garlic, crushed
1 teaspoon each
   chopped parsley
   and chives
salt and pepper
TO GARNISH:
few cooked whole
   prawns

Mix all the dressing ingredients together, seasoning with salt and pepper to taste; cover and set aside.

Arrange the endive or radicchio around the edge of individual plates or bowls. Mix together the crabmeat, prawns and lemon juice, and season well with salt and pepper. Skin, seed and chop the tomatoes and stir into the crab mixture.

Spoon the mixture into the centre of the plates and pour over the dressing. Garnish with the whole prawns.
Serves 4 to 6

Seafood Salad

4 scallops, quartered
16 mussels (see note)
350 g (12 oz)
　haddock fillets
150 ml (¼ pint) dry
　white wine
150 ml (¼ pint) fish
　stock
1 bay leaf
1 bouquet garni
salt and pepper
1 × 177 g (6 oz) can
　crabmeat, drained
DRESSING:
120 ml (4 fl oz)
　mayonnaise
1 tablespoon each
　chopped chives and
　parsley
1 clove garlic,
　crushed (optional)
2 eggs, hard-boiled
2 celery sticks
¼ cucumber, diced
TO SERVE:
2 small lettuce

Put the scallops, mussels and haddock in a shallow pan and pour over the wine and stock. Add the herbs and season well with salt and pepper. Bring to the boil and cook for 4 minutes, until the mussel shells have opened and the haddock is tender. Carefully remove from the stock, discarding any mussels that have not opened. Remove the shells. Place all the fish in a bowl, cover and leave to cool.

Put the mayonnaise, herbs and garlic (if using) in a mixing bowl, and season well with salt and pepper. Chop the eggs and celery and add to the bowl with the cucumber.

Add the crabmeat to the cooled fish, then spoon over the dressing and mix well. Arrange the lettuce in individual serving dishes and pile the fish mixture in the centre to serve.
Serves 4 to 6
NOTE: Canned mussels can be used in place of fresh ones; add them to the salad with the crabmeat.

Egg, Croûton and Cress Salad

6 slices white bread
oil for shallow-frying
4 eggs, hard-boiled
2 bunches watercress
2 mustard and cress
4 spring onions
1 green pepper, cored
    and seeded
salt and pepper
DRESSING:
50 g (2 oz) blue Brie
    cheese, softened
2 tablespoons each
    mayonnaise and
    double cream
1 tablespoon each
    chopped parsley
    and chives
pinch of cayenne
    pepper

Cut the bread into cubes. Heat the oil in a frying pan, add the bread and fry until golden brown. Drain on kitchen paper.

Chop the eggs and place in a large salad bowl. Break the watercress into sprigs and add to the bowl with the mustard and cress. Chop the spring onions and pepper; add to the bowl. Season well with salt and pepper.

To make the dressing, place the cheese in a bowl and beat until smooth. Gradually mix in the mayonnaise and cream, then fold in the herbs and cayenne. Season with salt to taste.

Spoon the dressing over the salad. Add the croûtons, toss well and serve immediately.
Serves 4

Piquant Winter Salad

500 g (1 lb) small
    waxy potatoes
1 small onion
2 celery sticks
2 carrots, grated
2 heads chicory
125 g (4 oz) ham
50 g (2 oz) salami
salt and pepper
DRESSING:
142 ml (5 fl oz)
    soured cream
2 tablespoons
    mayonnaise
2 tablespoons
    chopped chives
1 teaspoon made
    mustard
2 tablespoons green
    peppercorns
1 tablespoon chopped
    parsley
3 hard-boiled eggs

Cook the potatoes in their skins in boiling salted water for 15 to 20 minutes, until tender. Drain, then carefully remove the skins. Slice the potatoes and place in a salad bowl. Chop the onion and celery and add to the bowl with the carrots. Reserve a few chicory leaves for garnish. Slice the remaining chicory and ham; dice the salami. Add to the bowl with salt and pepper to taste and toss well.

To make the dressing, mix the soured cream, mayonnaise, chives, mustard, peppercorns and parsley. Season with salt and pepper to taste.

Cut the eggs in half and separate the whites from the yolks. Chop the whites and add to the dressing. Spoon over the salad and toss lightly.

Press the egg yolks through a sieve and sprinkle over the salad. Garnish with the chicory leaves to serve.
Serves 4

Saffron Salad

2 cloves garlic
1 teaspoon French
   mustard
1 teaspoon clear honey
5 tablespoons olive
   oil
2 tablespoons lemon
   or lime juice
salt and pepper
1 tablespoon each
   chopped parsley
   and chives
125 g (4 oz) raisins
2 onions, chopped
250 g (8 oz)
   long-grain rice
pinch of saffron strands
300 ml (½ pint) stock
50 g (2 oz) each
   salted peanuts and
   cashew nuts
125 g (4 oz) streaky
   bacon, derinded
lemon or lime slices
   to garnish

Slice 1 garlic clove and set aside; crush the other clove and place in a salad bowl with the mustard and honey. Stir in 4 tablespoons of the oil and the lemon or lime juice. Season well with salt and pepper. Stir in the parsley, chives and raisins.

Heat the remaining oil in a pan, add the sliced garlic and the onions and fry until browned. Stir in the rice, saffron and stock. Season with salt to taste, bring to the boil and cook for 12 minutes. Drain and leave to cool, then stir into the oil and lemon juice mixture with the nuts.

Cook the bacon under a preheated hot grill until crisp. Crumble and sprinkle over the rice. Garnish with lemon or lime slices.

Serves 4

NOTE: Use well-flavoured vegetable or chicken stock.

Pepper and Salami Salad

2 each large green,
  red and yellow
  peppers
6 tomatoes
4 hard-boiled eggs
50 g (2 oz) each
  garlic sausage and
  French salami
2 × 50 g (1¾ oz)
  cans anchovy
  fillets, drained
24 black olives
DRESSING:
2 cloves garlic, crushed
1 tablespoon each
  chopped parsley,
  chives, tarragon
  and chervil
1 teaspoon Meaux
  mustard
1 teaspoon clear honey
3 tablespoons lemon
  juice
6 tablespoons olive oil
salt and pepper

Place the whole peppers under a
preheated hot grill until the skins are
charred. Leave to cool, then peel
away the skin, remove the cores and
seeds, and slice the flesh.

Thickly slice the tomatoes and
eggs and arrange in a salad bowl.
Chop the garlic sausage and salami
and sprinkle into the bowl. Place the
peppers around the edge.

Arrange the anchovy fillets in a
lattice over the salad and place the
olives on top.

Mix the dressing ingredients
together in a bowl, seasoning with
salt and pepper to taste. Spoon over
the salad.

Chill for 20 minutes before
serving.
Serves 4

Chef's Salad

250 g (8 oz) spinach
125 g (4 oz)
   Gruyère cheese
125 g (4 oz) cooked
   chicken breast
125 g (4 oz) ham
125 g (4 oz) rare
   roast beef
1 tomato
2 eggs, hard-boiled
few stuffed olives
few basil leaves,
   chopped
1 tablespoon chopped
   parsley
DRESSING:
2 tablespoons lemon
   juice
4 tablespoons olive oil
1 teaspoon French
   mustard
1 teaspoon clear honey
2 teaspoons chopped
   thyme
2 tablespoons ground
   hazelnuts
salt and pepper

Break the spinach into small pieces
and arrange in a salad bowl or on a
flat plate.

Cut the cheese, chicken, ham and
beef into 5 cm (2 inch) strips and
arrange in sections on top of the
spinach.

Slice the tomato, eggs and olives
and arrange in the centre. Sprinkle
over the basil and parsley.

Mix all the dressing ingredients
together, seasoning with salt and
pepper to taste, and spoon over the
salad.

Serve immediately.
Serves 4

Chicken Salad with Grapes

125 g (4 oz) walnuts
125 g (4 oz) green
  grapes, seeded
500 g (1 lb) cooked
  chicken, shredded
2 tablespoons
  chopped tarragon
1 crisp lettuce
DRESSING:
1 clove garlic, crushed
4 spring onions,
  chopped
150 ml (¼ pint)
  mayonnaise
pinch of paprika
1 teaspoon curry
  powder
dash each of Tabasco
  and Worcestershire
  sauces
1 tablespoon finely
  chopped stuffed
  olives
salt and pepper
TO GARNISH:
few grapes
tarragon sprigs

First, make the dressing. Put the
garlic, spring onions, mayonnaise,
paprika and curry powder in a bowl
and mix well. Stir in the Tabasco and
Worcestershire sauces and olives, and
season with salt and pepper to taste.
Cover and leave to stand for at least
1 hour.

Roughly chop the walnuts and
halve the grapes. Place in a bowl
with the chicken and sprinkle over
the tarragon; stir well. Spoon over
the dressing and toss well to coat.

Arrange the lettuce leaves in a
salad bowl or on a plate. Spoon the
chicken salad on top and garnish
with grapes and tarragon.

Serve chilled.
Serves 4 to 6

Country Trout

2 tablespoons lemon
  or lime juice
1 tablespoon each
  chopped parsley,
  thyme and chives
1 shallot, very finely
  chopped
25 g (1 oz) butter,
  softened
salt and pepper
4 rainbow trout,
  cleaned
4 rashers streaky
  bacon, derinded
4 lemon or lime slices
4 rosemary sprigs

Mix together the lemon or lime juice, herbs, shallot, butter and salt and pepper to taste. Divide the mixture into 4 portions and spread into the cavities of the trout. Secure with cocktail sticks or sew up.

Wrap a rasher of bacon around each trout. Place each fish on a piece of foil, top with a lemon or lime slice and a rosemary sprig and wrap securely in the foil. Cook under a preheated moderate grill, or on a barbecue grid 10 cm (4 inches) above the coals, for 10 minutes each side.

Serve in the foil, with jacket potatoes and a green salad.
Serves 4

Herbed Chicken in Foil

2 tablespoons French
  mustard
3 tablespoons natural
  yogurt
6 chicken breasts
salt and pepper
2 tablespoons each
  chopped parsley,
  thyme and chervil
1 tablespoon chopped
  basil
grated rind of ½ lime
  or lemon
juice of 1 lime or
  lemon
lime or lemon slices
  to garnish

Mix the mustard and yogurt together and use to coat the chicken. Place each piece of chicken in the centre of a large piece of lightly oiled foil. Season well with salt and pepper, scatter a thick layer of herbs over the top and sprinkle with the lime or lemon rind and juice.

Wrap the foil securely around the chicken. Cook on the barbecue grid, about 15 cm (6 inches) above the coals, for 30 to 35 minutes, until tender. Alternatively, cook in a preheated moderately hot oven, 190°C (375°F), Gas Mark 5, for 25 minutes.

Serve in the foil, garnished with lime or lemon slices and accompanied by French bread.
Serves 6

Spicy Beefburgers

1 kg (2 lb) minced
    beef
salt
2 tablespoons green
    peppercorns
1 tablespoon chopped
    thyme
2 teaspoons Worcester-
    shire sauce
2 teaspoons French
    mustard
TO SERVE:
8 burger buns
8 lettuce leaves
selection of relishes
1 onion, sliced
4 tomatoes, sliced

Put the beef in a bowl and season
well with salt. Stir in the peppercorns,
thyme, Worcestershire sauce and
mustard; mix well. Divide into
8 portions and form into flat cakes.

Cook under a preheated moderate
grill, or on the barbecue grid 10 cm
(4 inches) above the coals, for 3 to
5 minutes each side, according to
taste.

Cut the buns in half and toast the
cut side. Arrange a lettuce leaf on
each bun base, top with a burger and
relish. Arrange onion and tomato
slices on top and replace the bun lid.
Serve immediately, in a napkin.
Serves 4 to 8

Winchester Sausages

Sausages are the perfect brunch or barbecue food and
these are well worth making.

250 g (8 oz) belly
    pork, minced
250 g (8 oz) lean
    minced pork
25 g (1 oz) pork fat,
    minced
6 tablespoons milk
75 g (3 oz) whole-
    meal breadcrumbs
1 clove garlic, crushed
¼ teaspoon each
    ground mace and
    allspice
1 tablespoon each
    chopped parsley
    and sage
1 teaspoon chopped
    thyme
salt and pepper
about 1 metre (3 ft)
    sausage casing (see
    note)

Mix the pork and fat together in a
bowl. Pour the milk over the
breadcrumbs and leave for 10
minutes. Squeeze the breadcrumbs
dry and add to the meat. Add the
garlic, spices, herbs, and salt and
pepper to taste and mix well.

Using a piping bag fitted with a
large plain nozzle, carefully force the
sausage mixture into the casings.
Push the mixture evenly along the
casing then twist to form sausages.

Cook under a preheated moderate
grill or on the barbecue grid, 10 cm
(4 inches) above the coals, for 15 to
20 minutes, until golden brown and
thoroughly cooked.
Makes about 10 to 12
NOTE: Sausage casings are available
from some butchers. They should be
soaked overnight in cold water and
drained before use.

Spareribs with Ginger

1 kg (2 lb) pork
   spareribs
SAUCE:
2 spring onions,
   chopped
2 cloves garlic, thinly
   sliced
2.5 cm (1 inch) piece
   ginger root,
   shredded
1 tablespoon soy
   sauce
4 tablespoons clear
   honey
3 tablespoons lemon
   juice
2 tablespoons mango
   chutney
1/2 teaspoon ground
   ginger
1 tablespoon oil
2 tablespoons dry
   sherry

Put the spareribs in a roasting pan,
cover and cook in a preheated
moderately hot oven, 200°C (400°F),
Gas Mark 6, for 30 minutes, or on
the barbecue grid 10 cm (4 inches)
above the coals.

Put all the sauce ingredients in a
pan over a low heat, gradually bring
to the boil and cook for 1 minute.

Pour off the fat and liquid from
the roasting pan. Spoon the sauce
over the ribs, covering them all well.

Return to the oven or barbecue
and cook for 15 to 20 minutes,
basting frequently.

Serve hot or cold.

Serves 4 to 6

Seafood Kebabs

250 g (8 oz) plaice
    fillets
4 sardines or other
    small fish
8 large cooked
    unshelled prawns
4 scallops, halved
8 rashers streaky
    bacon, derinded
few bay leaves
few lemon wedges
MARINADE:
juice of 1 lemon
4 tablespoons olive oil
1 bouquet garni
salt and pepper
SAUCE:
6 tablespoons
    mayonnaise
1 clove garlic, crushed
1 teaspoon tomato
    purée
dash of Tabasco sauce
1 tablespoon each
    chopped parsley,
    thyme and capers

Cut the plaice into chunks and the sardines into halves.

Mix the marinade ingredients together with salt and pepper to taste, add all the fish and mix well. Leave to marinate for 30 minutes, stirring occasionally.

Put the sauce ingredients in a bowl and mix well. Spoon into a serving dish, cover and set aside.

Drain the marinade from the fish and reserve. Cut the bacon rashers in half and roll up. Arrange the fish alternately on skewers with the bacon, interspersing with bay leaves and lemon wedges to taste. Cook under a preheated moderate grill, or on a barbecue grid 10 cm (4 inches) above the coals, for 5 to 7 minutes on each side, basting with the marinade.

Serve hot, with the sauce.
Serves 8

Pâté-Filled Croissants

500 (1 lb) strong
  white plain flour
2 teaspoons salt
25 g (1 oz) lard
15 g (½ oz) dried
  yeast
1 teaspoon caster
  sugar
175 ml (6 fl oz)
  warm water
1 egg, beaten
175 g (6 oz) butter,
  softened
175 g (6 oz) smooth
  pâté, softened
beaten egg to glaze

Sift the flour and salt into a bowl. Rub in the lard until the mixture resembles fine breadcrumbs.

Combine the yeast, sugar and warm water. Leave in a warm place for about 10 minutes, then add to the flour with the beaten egg and mix to a smooth dough. Turn onto a floured surface and knead for about 10 minutes, until smooth. Roll out to a 45 × 15 cm (18 × 6 inch) rectangle.

Divide the butter into 3 portions. Spread one-third over the top two-thirds of the dough. Fold the lower, uncovered third of dough up over the centre and the top down over both. Seal the edges with a rolling pin and give the dough a half-turn. Leave to rest in the refrigerator for 10 minutes. Repeat the rolling, folding and resting process with the remaining butter; cover and leave to rest in the refrigerator for 30 minutes after the final folding.

Roll out to a 45 × 30 cm (18 × 12 inch) rectangle. Trim the edges and cut the dough in half lengthways. Cut each strip into 6 triangles, the base of each 15 cm (6 inches) long.

Spoon a little pâté onto the centre of each triangle and brush the edges with beaten egg. Roll each croissant loosely, starting at the wide side and rolling up towards the point; shape into crescents. Place on baking sheets, cover loosely with a plastic bag and leave in a warm place for 30 minutes, until slightly risen.

Brush with beaten egg and bake in a preheated hot oven, 220°C (425°F), Gas Mark 7, for 20 minutes, until well risen and golden. Serve hot.
Makes 12
NOTE: If only half this quantity is required, the remainder can be kept in a freezer for up to 3 months.

Tomato and Herb Tarts

175 g (6 oz) plain
    flour
pinch of salt
65 g (2½ oz)
    matured Cheddar
    cheese
1 tablespoon grated
    Parmesan cheese
3 egg yolks
100 g (3½ oz)
    butter, softened
FILLING:
350 g (12 oz)
    tomatoes, skinned
    and sliced
2 tablespoons each
    chopped parsley,
    basil and thyme
50 g (2 oz) Gruyère
    cheese, sliced

Sift the flour and salt onto a board.
Make a well in the centre; add the
cheeses, egg yolks and butter, and
gradually work into the flour. Knead
until smooth, form into a ball, cover
and chill for 1 hour.

Roll out and use to line eight 7.5 cm
(3 inch) tartlet tins. Chill for 20 minutes. Line with greaseproof paper and
dried beans and bake blind in a preheated moderately hot oven, 200°C
(400°F), Gas Mark 6, for 20 minutes.
Remove the paper and beans and
return to the oven for 5 minutes.

Layer the tomato slices in the
pastry cases, sprinkling each layer
with herbs. Top with the cheese.
Return to the oven for 5 minutes,
until the cheese is bubbling. Leave to
cool in the tins. Serve cold.
Makes 8

51

Summer Pâté

40 g (1½ oz) butter
4 spring onions,
  chopped
1 celery stick, finely
  chopped
1 × 198 g (7 oz)
  can tuna fish,
  drained
2 tomatoes, skinned,
  seeded and roughly
  chopped
2 tablespoons
  mayonnaise
2 teaspoons lemon
  juice
salt and pepper
1 tablespoon green
  peppercorns,
  drained

Melt the butter in a pan, add the spring onions and celery and cook for 5 minutes, without browning. Leave to cool, then place in a blender or food processor with the tuna, tomatoes, mayonnaise, lemon juice, and salt and pepper to taste; blend until smooth. Stir in the peppercorns.

Turn into a serving dish or picnic container. Serve with crusty bread or melba toast.

Serves 4 to 6

Chicken Tarragon Pâté

8 rashers streaky
   bacon, derinded
500 g (1 lb) chicken,
   diced
250 g (8 oz) belly
   pork, minced
125 g (4 oz) pork
   fat, diced
1 onion, finely chopped
1 clove garlic, crushed
1 tablespoon green
   peppercorns
3 tablespoons brandy
   or dry sherry
3 tablespoons dry
   vermouth or dry
   white wine
1 small egg, beaten
1-2 tablespoons
   chopped tarragon
salt and pepper

Using the back of a knife, stretch the bacon rashers and use to line the base and sides of a 1 kg (2 lb) loaf tin or similar ovenproof dish.

Mix the remaining ingredients together; season very well with salt and pepper. Turn into the prepared tin and smooth the top.

Cover with lightly buttered greaseproof paper and foil and place in a roasting pan half-filled with hot water. Cook in a preheated moderate oven, 160°C (325°F), Gas Mark 3, for 2 to 2¼ hours.

Leave to cool in the tin for 1 hour, then place a weight on top of the pâté. Leave until completely cold, before removing the weight.

Serve from the tin on a picnic, or turn out onto a serving dish.
Serves 6 to 8

Raised Chicken and Ham Pie

PASTRY:
125 g (4 oz) lard
150 ml (¼ pint)
water
150 ml (¼ pint)
milk
2 teaspoons salt
500 g (1 lb) plain
flour, sifted
beaten egg to glaze
FILLING:
1 × 1.5 kg (3½ lb)
oven-ready chicken
250 g (8 oz) lean
bacon, derinded
and diced
250 g (8 oz) streaky
bacon, derinded
and minced
350 g (12 oz)
minced veal
1 onion, minced or
finely chopped
2 tablespoons
chopped parsley
1 tablespoon each
chopped thyme
and sage
4 tablespoons dry
white wine or
sherry
salt and pepper
TO FINISH:
15 g (½ oz) aspic
jelly crystals

Put the lard, water, milk and salt in a large saucepan and bring to the boil. Remove from the heat, add all the flour and quickly mix together to form a smooth dough. Knead lightly.

Turn onto a floured surface and roll out two-thirds to a circle about 30 cm (12 inches) in diameter. Fold the circle in quarters and use to line a deep 15 cm (6 inch) round loose-bottomed cake tin, unfolding and shaping in the tin; leave the dough overlapping the edge.

Remove the skin and bones from the chicken. Cut the breast meat into strips and dice the rest of the flesh. Mix with the bacon, veal, onion, herbs, wine or sherry, and plenty of salt and pepper. Turn into the tin, smoothing the top.

Roll out the remaining pastry for a lid, dampen the edges, put in position and seal, trim and flute. Make a hole in the centre of the pie and decorate with the pastry trimmings.

Brush with beaten egg and bake in a preheated moderately hot oven, 200°C (400°F), Gas Mark 6, for 30 minutes. Lower the temperature to 180°C (350°F), Gas Mark 4, and bake for 2 hours. Leave to cool in the tin.

Make up 300 ml (½ pint) aspic jelly from the crystals, according to packet directions, and leave to cool slightly. Put a funnel in the hole in the pie and carefully pour in the jelly. Leave until cold and set before cutting.
Serves 6 to 8

Potted Kippers

2 pairs smoked
  kippers
150 g (5 oz)
  unsalted butter
grated rind and juice
  of ½ lemon
pepper
142 ml (5 fl oz)
  double cream,
  lightly whipped
few lemon slices
25 g (1 oz) butter,
  clarified (see below)

Dot the kippers with half the unsalted butter. Cook under a preheated moderate grill for 3 to 4 minutes on each side, basting occasionally.

Cool slightly, then remove the skin and bones. Place the flesh in a blender or food processor with the remaining unsalted butter and blend until smooth. Stir in the lemon juice and rind, and pepper to taste. Fold in the cream and transfer to a serving dish.

Spoon over the clarified butter and chill in the refrigerator until set.

Serve with crusty bread and lettuce.

Serves 4 to 6

TO CLARIFY BUTTER: Melt, allow to settle, then strain through muslin.

Cheese and Onion Plait

500 g (1 lb) strong
    white plain flour
2 teaspoons salt
25 g (1 oz) butter
2 teaspoons dried
    yeast
1 teaspoon caster
    sugar
scant 300 ml (½ pint)
    lukewarm milk
1 egg, beaten
FILLING:
1 tablespoon oil
2 large onions,
    chopped
125 g (4 oz)
    matured Cheddar
    cheese, grated
TO FINISH:
beaten egg
25 g (1 oz) flaked
    almonds (optional)
pinch of salt
    (optional)

Sift the flour and salt into a bowl and rub in the butter until the mixture resembles fine breadcrumbs.

Combine the yeast, sugar and warm milk and leave in a warm place for about 10 minutes.

Add the yeast mixture and beaten egg to the flour and mix to a smooth dough. Turn onto a floured surface and knead for about 10 minutes, until the dough is smooth and not sticky. Cover and leave to rise in a warm place for about 1¼ hours, or until doubled in size.

Meanwhile, heat the oil in a pan, add the onions and fry until golden brown; leave to cool.

Knock back the dough and mix in the fried onions and grated cheese, making sure they are evenly distributed. Divide the dough in half, then divide each half into 3 equal portions. Roll each portion with the hands into 30–35 cm (12–14 inch) long ropes. Plait 3 pieces together and pinch the ends to secure. Repeat with the other 3 pieces.

Place each loaf on a baking sheet, cover with a plastic bag and leave in a warm place to rise for about 40 to 45 minutes.

Brush with beaten egg and bake in a preheated moderately hot oven, 200°C (400°F), Gas Mark 6, for 20 minutes. Brush again with egg and sprinkle with the almonds and salt, if using. Return to the oven for 20 to 25 minutes, until well risen and golden brown.

Cool on a wire rack. Serve with butter, and cheese if liked.

Makes 2 plaits

Crunchy Wholewheat Bread

125 g (4 oz) butter
50 g (2 oz) soft
brown sugar
2 tablespoons black
treacle
1 egg, beaten
125 g (4 oz) strong
white plain flour
1 teaspoon each
bicarbonate of soda
and baking powder
125 g (4 oz)
wholewheat flour
good pinch of salt
2 × 150 g (5.2 oz)
cartons natural
yogurt
175 g (6 oz) muesli

Cream the butter and sugar together until light and fluffy. Gradually beat in the treacle and egg.

Sift the plain flour, bicarbonate of soda and baking powder together into a bowl, then stir in the wholewheat flour and salt.

Gradually fold the flour mixture and yogurt alternately into the creamed mixture. Fold in the muesli.

Turn into a greased 1 kg (2 lb) loaf tin and smooth the top. Bake in a preheated moderate oven, 180°C (350°F), Gas Mark 4, for 1 hour, until well risen and golden brown. Cool on a wire rack.

Serve sliced and buttered.
Makes one 1 kg (2 lb) loaf

57

Spicy Rock Cakes

250 g (8 oz)
  self-raising flour
125 g (4 oz) sugar
125 g (4 oz) soft
  margarine
½ teaspoon each
  ground nutmeg
  and mixed spice
1 large egg, beaten
little milk
50 g (2 oz) raisins

Sift the flour into a bowl, stir in the sugar, then rub in the margarine until the mixture resembles breadcrumbs. Stir in the spices and gradually add the egg and enough milk to give a fairly stiff consistency. Fold in the raisins. Place in rough mounds on 2 greased baking sheets.

Bake in a preheated moderate oven, 180°C (350°F), Gas Mark 4, for 15 to 20 minutes, until golden brown.

Cool on a wire rack.

Makes 18

Candied Curd Tart

250 g (8 oz) plain
  flour
pinch of salt
75 g (3 oz) caster
  sugar
125 g (4 oz) butter
grated rind of
  ½ lemon
2 egg yolks
FILLING:
175 g (6 oz) cream
  cheese
175 g (6 oz) curd
  cheese
75 g (3 oz) caster
  sugar
grated rind of
  1 lemon
grated rind of
  1 orange
125 g (4 oz) candied
  peel
50 g (2 oz) ground
  almonds
3 eggs, beaten
TO FINISH:
icing sugar, sifted

Sift the flour and salt into a large mixing bowl, then stir in the sugar. Rub in the butter until the mixture resembles fine breadcrumbs. Stir in the lemon rind, then gradually knead in the egg yolks. Knead lightly until well mixed. Wrap in greaseproof paper and chill for 1 hour.

Roll out on a floured surface and use to line an 18 cm (7 inch) fluted flan ring placed on a baking sheet. Chill for 30 minutes.

Meanwhile, make the filling. Beat the cheeses, sugar and fruit rinds together, then stir in the peel and almonds. Gradually stir in the eggs. Spoon the mixture into the pastry case. Roll out the pastry trimmings, cut into strips and use to make a criss-cross pattern over the top of the flan.

Bake in a preheated moderate oven, 180°C (350°F), Gas Mark 4, for 40 to 45 minutes, until golden brown.

Serve cold, sprinkled with icing sugar.

Serves 8

PACKED MEALS

Crunchy Chicken Drumsticks

50 g (2 oz) fresh
  white breadcrumbs
1 tablespoon each
  chopped parsley
  and chives
1 tablespoon grated
  Parmesan cheese
2 tablespoons
  blanched almonds,
  chopped
8 chicken drumsticks
salt and pepper
1 egg, beaten
50 g (2 oz) butter
2 cloves garlic,
  crushed

Mix the breadcrumbs, parsley, chives, Parmesan cheese and almonds together. Season the drumsticks with salt and pepper, dip into the beaten egg and coat with the breadcrumb mixture.

Melt the butter in a pan, add the garlic and cook for 1 minute, without browning.

Place the drumsticks in a roasting pan, spoon over the garlic butter and cook in a preheated moderate oven, 180°C (350°F), Gas Mark 4, for 35 to 40 minutes, basting occasionally, until well cooked and golden brown. Serve hot or cold.

Serves 4

Herbed Scotch Eggs

250 g (8 oz) sausage
  meat
1 teaspoon Worcester-
  shire sauce
1 tablespoon chopped
  parsley
1 teaspoon dried
  mixed herbs
salt and pepper
2 teaspoons made
  mustard
1 tablespoon plain
  flour
salt and pepper
4 eggs, hard-boiled
1 egg, beaten
dried breadcrumbs
oil for deep-frying

Put the sausage meat in a bowl. Stir in the Worcestershire sauce and herbs, and season well with salt and pepper. Divide the mixture into 4 portions and form each into a flat cake. Spread with mustard.

Season the flour with salt and pepper and use to coat the eggs. Press the sausage meat evenly around the eggs, making sure there are no cracks in the surface. Dip in the beaten egg and breadcrumbs.

Heat the oil and deep-fry the eggs for 7 to 8 minutes, until golden brown and crisp. Drain on kitchen paper and leave to cool.
Makes 4

Traditional Cornish Pasties

1 × 370 g (13 oz)
  packet frozen puff
  pastry, thawed
350 g (12 oz) very
  lean chuck or skirt
  steak, diced
4 potatoes, diced
2 large onions,
  chopped
1-2 teaspoons dried
  mixed herbs
salt and pepper
beaten egg to glaze

Divide the pastry into 4 pieces and roll out each piece into a 15–18 cm (6–7 inch) circle; trim to neaten.

Mix the meat, potatoes and onions together, stir in the herbs and season very well with salt and pepper.

Divide into 4 portions and spoon into the centre of the pastry rounds. Dampen the edges and fold over into the centre. Pinch and crimp the edges, sealing well. Place on a baking sheet and chill for 30 minutes.

Brush with beaten egg and bake in a preheated hot oven, 220°C (425°F), Gas Mark 7, for 30 to 45 minutes, until risen and golden brown.

Serve hot or cold.

Makes 4

Granary Croustades

8 large slices day-old
  granary bread
25-50 g (1-2 oz)
  butter
FILLING:
1 × 198 g (7 oz)
  can tuna, drained
1 celery stick, diced
1 tablespoon stuffed
  olives, chopped
1 egg, hard-boiled
  and chopped
3 tablespoons
  mayonnaise
2 spring onions,
  chopped
squeeze of lemon
  juice
1 tablespoon chopped
  parsley
TO GARNISH:
stuffed olives, sliced

Remove the crusts from the bread and trim each slice into a large circle. Melt the butter and brush all over the bread. Fit each round into 8 patty tins, shaping up the sides. Bake in a preheated moderate oven, 180°C (350°F), Gas Mark 4, for 30 to 45 minutes, until very crisp and golden brown. Remove from the patty tins and cool on a wire rack.

Mix the filling ingredients together and spoon into the croustades. Top with olive slices.
Makes 8

Egg and Bacon Pies

PASTRY:
175 g (6 oz) plain
*   flour*
pinch of salt
40 g (1½ oz) lard
40 g (1½ oz) butter
little iced water to
*   mix*

FILLING:
5 eggs, beaten
200 ml (⅓ pint)
*   single cream*
little grated nutmeg
salt and pepper
175 g (6 oz) back
*   bacon, derinded*
*   and diced*
4 spring onions,
*   chopped*

Sift the flour and salt into a bowl and rub in the lard and butter until the mixture resembles breadcrumbs. Add enough water to give a firm dough. Knead lightly, wrap in cling film and chill for 30 minutes. Roll out on a floured surface and use to line six 10 cm (4 inch) tins.

Mix together the eggs, cream, nutmeg, and salt and pepper to taste.

Divide the bacon between the pastry cases. Sprinkle with the spring onions and pour in the egg mixture.

Bake in a preheated moderate oven, 180°C (350°F), Gas Mark 4, for 25 minutes, until golden brown. Remove from the tins and cool on a wire rack. Serve with salad.
Makes 6

Sausage and Bacon Rolls

PASTRY:
175 g (6 oz) plain
*   flour*
pinch of salt
40 g (1½ oz) butter
40 g (1½ oz) lard
little iced water to
*   mix*
beaten egg to glaze

FILLING:
125 g (4 oz) streaky
*   bacon, derinded*
250 g (8 oz) sausage
*   meat*
1 teaspoon dried
*   mixed herbs*
salt and pepper
little flour

Sift the flour and salt into a bowl and rub in the fats until the mixture resembles breadcrumbs. Add enough water to make a fairly stiff dough. Knead lightly, wrap in cling film and chill for 30 minutes.

Roll out into a 30 × 15 cm (12 × 6 inch) oblong, then cut in half lengthways. Lay the bacon on top.

Mix the sausage meat and herbs together with salt and pepper to taste. Divide in half and dust with flour, then form into 2 rolls the length of the pastry and place down the centre of each strip. Brush the edges with beaten egg, fold one side over the sausage meat and press the edges together, sealing well. Cut into 5 cm (2 inch) lengths.

Place on a baking sheet and bake in a preheated moderate oven, 180°C (350°F), Gas Mark 4, for 25 minutes, until golden. Serve hot or cold.
Makes 12

Old-Fashioned Game Pie

FILLING:

350 g (12 oz) boneless rabbit, diced

350 g (12 oz) belly of pork, minced

350 g (12 oz) pheasant, diced

175 g (6 oz) streaky bacon, derinded and chopped

1 tablespoon chopped parsley

1 teaspoon chopped sage

1 teaspoon dried mixed herbs

pinch of ground mace

2 tablespoons green peppercorns (optional)

salt and pepper

4 tablespoons brandy or dry sherry

PASTRY:

625 g (1¼ lb) plain flour

2 teaspoons salt

150 g (5 oz) lard

150 ml (¼ pint) water

150 ml (¼ pint) milk

beaten egg to glaze

JELLIED STOCK:

1 × 425 g (15 oz) can consommé

1 teaspoon gelatine

Put the meats, herbs, mace, peppercorns, if using, and salt and pepper to taste in a large bowl. Pour over the brandy or sherry and mix well. Cover and set aside.

Sift the flour and salt into a bowl. Put the lard, water and milk in a pan, bring just to the boil, pour into the bowl and mix well. Knead lightly.

Cut off one third of the dough, cover with foil and keep on one side for the lid. Roll out the remaining dough on a floured surface to a 35 cm (14 inch) circle. Fold in quarters and use to line a deep 18 cm (7 inch) round loose-bottomed cake tin, unfolding and shaping round the tin and leaving the dough overlapping the edge. Spoon in the meat mixture.

Roll out the remaining dough, dampen the edge and use to cover the pie, sealing the edges well. Trim off excess pastry and pinch or flute the edges. Make a hole in the centre of the pie. Roll out the trimmings and use to decorate the pie.

Brush with beaten egg and bake in a preheated moderately hot oven, 200°C (400°F), Gas Mark 6, for 30 minutes. Lower the temperature to 180°C (350°F), Gas Mark 4, and bake for 2 hours; cover with foil if the top browns too quickly. Leave in the tin until completely cold.

Place the consommé in a pan, sprinkle over the gelatine and heat gently, stirring, until dissolved. Remove from the heat and leave until just on the point of setting, then pour through the hole in the pie, using a funnel.

Leave for 2 to 3 hours until set, then remove from the tin. Serve chilled, with salad.

Serves 6 to 8

Brittany Crêpes

BATTER:
250 g (8 oz)
   wholemeal flour
good pinch of salt
2 eggs
300 ml (½ pint)
   milk
150 ml (¼ pint)
   water
oil for frying
FILLING:
1 tablespoon oil
2 cloves garlic, thinly
   sliced
1 large onion, sliced
1 green pepper, cored,
   seeded and sliced
1 aubergine, chopped
350 g (12 oz)
   tomatoes, skinned
   and sliced
1 teaspoon dried
   mixed herbs
1 tablespoon chopped
   parsley
salt and pepper
2 tablespoons grated
   Parmesan cheese

Put the flour and salt in a bowl, make a well in the centre and add the eggs, milk and water. Beat to make a smooth batter. Leave for 30 minutes.

Heat a little oil in a 15 cm (6 inch) heavy-based frying pan and pour in just enough batter to cover the base. Cook for 2 to 3 minutes until the underside is brown; turn and cook the other side until golden. Place on a piece of greaseproof paper and cover with a tea-towel. Repeat with remaining batter to make 10 to 12 crêpes.

To make the filling, heat the oil in a pan, add the garlic and onion and cook gently for 5 minutes. Add the remaining ingredients, except the Parmesan, seasoning well with salt and pepper. Cook for 15 to 20 minutes. Stir in the Parmesan.

Divide the filling between the crêpes and roll up, tucking under the ends. Place on a greased baking sheet and bake in a preheated hot oven, 200°C (400°F), Gas Mark 6, for 30 to 35 minutes, until crisp. Serve hot or cold.
Makes 10 to 12

Chicken and Nut Sandwich

4 boneless chicken
 breasts, cooked
4 pitta breads
2 celery sticks
5 cm (2 inch) piece
 cucumber
2 spring onions
25 g (1 oz) bean
 sprouts
2 tablespoons
 mayonnaise
2 tablespoons
 peanuts, chopped
1 tablespoon chopped
 parsley
squeeze of lemon
 juice
8 small lettuce leaves
2 tomatoes, sliced

Remove the skin from the chicken, dice the flesh and place in a bowl.

Warm the pitta bread, cut in half and open each half out to form 'pockets'.

Finely chop the celery, cucumber and spring onions; add to the chicken with the bean sprouts and mayonnaise. Stir in the peanuts, parsley and lemon juice.

Put a lettuce leaf in each pit bread half. Spoon in the chicke salad and top with tomato slice.
Makes 8

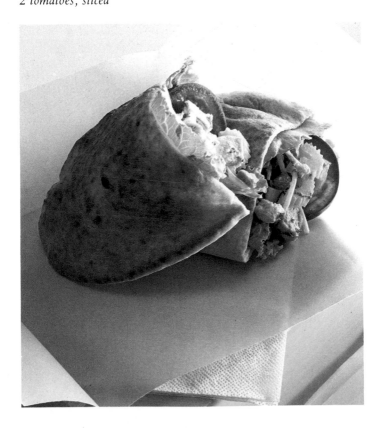

Club Sandwiches

4 slices white bread,
  crusts removed
2 tablespoons
  mayonnaise
4 slices buttered
  brown bread,
  crusts removed
2 teaspoons French
  mustard
175 g (6 oz) cooked
  chicken, thinly
  sliced
3 tomatoes, sliced
salt and pepper
4 lettuce leaves
mustard and cress

Spread the white bread with the mayonnaise and the brown bread with the mustard. Arrange the chicken on the brown bread, top with the tomatoes, and season well with salt and pepper. Put the lettuce on top, sprinkle over the mustard and cress, and sandwich with the white bread. Press well together and cut into quarters.

Makes 4 sandwiches

Ham and Tomato Double Decker Sandwich

125 g (4 oz) cream
  cheese with chives
8 slices brown bread
4 tomatoes, sliced
125 g (4 oz) ham,
  minced
1 teaspoon made
  mustard
2 tablespoons
  mayonnaise
4 lettuce leaves,
  shredded
4 slices buttered
  white bread

Spread cream cheese on one side of a brown bread slice. Cover with sliced tomato and another brown slice. Mix the ham, mustard and mayonnaise together and spread over the brown bread. Cover with lettuce then top with a slice of white bread. Press the sandwich well together and cut into quarters. Repeat with the remaining ingredients.

Makes 4 sandwiches

Crabmeat Sandwiches

1 × 177 g (6 oz)
  can crabmeat
squeeze of lemon
  juice
1-2 tablespoons
  mayonnaise
1 tablespoon chopped
  parsley
2 tablespoons
  chopped chives
salt and pepper
8 slices buttered
  brown bread
mustard and cress

Put the crabmeat in a bowl with the lemon juice, mayonnaise and herbs and mix well, seasoning with salt and pepper to taste.

Spread the crabmeat on 4 slices of bread. Sprinkle over the mustard and cress and top with the remaining bread. Cut the sandwiches into halves or quarters.

Makes 4 sandwiches

Fillet Steaks with Stilton

75 g (3 oz) blue
   Stilton cheese
75 g (3 oz) butter,
   softened
1 tablespoon port
1 teaspoon each
   chopped chives and
   thyme
½ clove garlic,
   crushed
salt and pepper
6 × 2.5 cm (1 inch)
   fillet steaks
thyme sprigs to
   garnish

Put the cheese, butter and port in a blender or food processor and blend until smooth. Stir in the herbs, garlic and salt and pepper to taste. Form the mixture into a roll, wrap in foil and chill in the ice compartment of the refrigerator for 20 minutes.

Season the steaks with salt and pepper and cook under a preheated hot grill for 3 to 5 minutes on each side, according to taste. Arrange on a warmed serving dish.

Cut the butter into 6 and place on the steaks. Garnish with thyme and serve immediately, with courgettes.
Serves 6

Involtini with Tomatoes

12 thin slices
  Mortadella
12 slices sirloin beef,
  each weighing 50 g
  (2 oz), beaten flat
2 tablespoons oil
1 clove garlic, thinly
  sliced
1 teaspoon dried
  thyme
150 ml (¼ pint) dry
  white wine
1 × 539 g (1 lb 3 oz)
  can tomatoes
1 × 64 g (2¼ oz)
  can tomato purée
1 tablespoon chopped
  basil
salt and pepper
bay or basil leaves to
  garnish

Lay a slice of Mortadella on each beef slice, roll into a sausage shape and secure with a cocktail stick. Heat the oil in a pan, add the meat and brown on all sides. Drain on kitchen paper.

Pour off the excess fat from the pan. Add the garlic and thyme, then stir in the wine and tomatoes, with their juice. Bring to the boil and boil rapidly for 10 minutes. Add the tomato purée and basil. Season to taste with salt and pepper.

Return the meat rolls to the pan, cover and cook for 35 to 40 minutes. Just before serving, increase the heat to reduce the sauce. Garnish with bay or basil.

Serve with a green vegetable and pasta, rice or bread.
Serves 6

Tagliatelle Pesto

4 cloves garlic
50 g (2 oz) basil
  leaves
75 g (3 oz)
  Parmesan cheese,
  freshly grated
5-6 tablespoons olive
  oil
550 g (1 lb 2 oz) egg
  tagliatelle

Put the garlic and basil in a mortar and pound together until smooth. When the ingredients are pulped, gradually add the cheese and continue pounding until the mixture becomes oily. Add the oil, drop by drop, until a smooth sauce is obtained.

Meanwhile, cook the pasta in boiling salted water for 7 to 9 minutes, or according to packet instructions. Drain well, return to the pan and pour over the pesto sauce, mixing well.

Transfer to a warmed serving dish and serve immediately, with extra Parmesan cheese.

Serves 4 to 6

NOTE: Ready-made pesto is available in jars.

Italian Veal Rolls

6 thin slices ham
6 veal escalopes, each
  weighing 50 g
  (2 oz), beaten flat
50 g (2 oz) pork fat,
  finely chopped
1 clove garlic, sliced
2 tablespoons pine nuts
2 tablespoons sultanas
2 tablespoons grated
  Parmesan cheese
3 tablespoons
  chopped parsley
6 slices Gruyère
  cheese
salt and pepper
1 tablespoon oil
300 ml (½ pint) dry
  white wine
1 tablespoon tomato
  purée

Lay a slice of ham on each escalope. Sprinkle with the pork fat, garlic, pine nuts, sultanas, Parmesan cheese and 1 tablespoon of the parsley. Top with the Gruyère cheese and season well with salt and pepper. Roll up and secure with cocktail sticks.

Heat the oil in a pan, add the veal rolls and brown on all sides. Pour over the wine, season well and bring to the boil. Cover and simmer for 25 to 30 minutes, until tender. Remove the rolls from the pan with a slotted spoon and arrange on a warmed serving dish. Keep warm.

Boil the liquid in the pan until reduced by half, then stir in the tomato purée and remaining parsley. Spoon the sauce over the veal rolls.

Serve with rice or noodles and a tossed green salad.

Serves 6

Pork Stuffed with Pâté

2 pork tenderloins
125 g (4 oz) smooth
  pâté
salt and pepper
25 g (1 oz) unsalted
  butter
1 clove garlic, crushed
50 g (2 oz)
  mushrooms,
  chopped
150 ml (¼ pint) dry
  sherry
150 ml (¼ pint) dry
  white wine
1 teaspoon French
  mustard
dash of Worcester-
  shire sauce
½ teaspoon mixed
  herbs
2 tablespoons double
  cream
2 tablespoons
  chopped chives
1 tablespoon capers
  (optional)

Using a sharp knife, make a horizontal
cut through the centre of the pork,
taking care not to cut right through.
Spread the pâté over the cut surface
and sew up, ensuring that the pâté is
enclosed. Season with salt and pepper.

Melt the butter in a large frying
pan, add the meat and brown on all
sides. Remove from the pan and
drain on kitchen paper.

Add the garlic to the pan and fry
until browned. Add the mushrooms
and cook for 1 minute. Add the
sherry, wine, mustard, Worcestershire sauce and herbs. Bring to the
boil, return the pork to the pan, cover
and simmer for 35 to 40 minutes,
turning occasionally. Remove the
pork from the pan; keep warm.

Increase the heat and boil the
liquid in the pan until thickened. Stir
in the cream, cook for 2 minutes.

Slice the pork and arrange on a
warmed serving dish. Add the chives
and capers, if using, to the sauce.
Spoon over the pork and serve
immediately, with a green vegetable.
Serves 4 to 6

Skewered Sicilian Pork

750 g (1½ lb) pork
   fillet
4 × 2.5 cm (1 inch)
   slices French
   bread, quartered
8 small slices Parma
   ham or streaky
   bacon rashers,
   halved and rolled up
sage and bay leaves
MARINADE:
4 tablespoons olive
   oil
2 tablespoons lemon
   juice
1 clove garlic, crushed
1 tablespoon mixed
   herbs
salt and pepper

Cut the pork into 2.5 cm (1 inch) cubes.

Put the marinade ingredients in a bowl, with salt and pepper to taste, and mix well. Add the pork cubes and marinade for 1 to 2 hours, turning occasionally. Remove the meat from the marinade with a slotted spoon; reserve the marinade.

Arrange the pork, French bread and Parma ham or bacon alternately on 8 skewers, interspersing with sage and bay leaves to taste.

Cook under a preheated moderate grill, or over a charcoal grill, for 10 minutes on each side, until the pork is tender and browned, basting with the remaining marinade during cooking.

Serve hot, with a green salad and selection of vegetables.
Serves 4 to 6

Beef Stroganoff

25 g (1 oz) butter
2 onions, sliced
1-2 cloves garlic,
  crushed
750 g (1½ lb) rump
  or sirloin steak
2 tablespoons dry red
  wine
125 g (4 oz) button
  mushrooms, sliced
1 teaspoon French
  mustard
150 g (5.2 oz)
  natural yogurt
salt and pepper
1 tablespoon each
  chopped thyme
  and parsley
croûtons of fried
  bread to serve

Melt the butter in a large frying pan,
add the onions and garlic and fry
until lightly browned. Cut the steak
into thin strips, add to the pan and
brown on all sides. Add the wine and
boil for 5 minutes, until the liquid
has reduced. Add the mushrooms,
mustard, yogurt, and salt and pepper
to taste and simmer for 5 minutes.

Just before serving, stir in the
herbs. Garnish with croûtons and
serve with noodles.
Serves 4

Lamb Cutlets with Sherry Sauce

8 lamb cutlets
1 clove garlic, sliced
1 egg, beaten
50 g (2 oz) white
* breadcrumbs*
1-2 tablespoons oil
25 g (1 oz) unsalted
* butter*
1 tablespoon each
* chopped thyme,*
* parsley, sage and*
* chives*
150 ml (¼ pint) dry
* sherry*
142 ml (5 fl oz)
* double cream*
salt and pepper
TO GARNISH:
125 g (4 oz) green
* olives*
sage leaves

Cut small slits in the cutlets and push in the slivered garlic. Coat each cutlet with egg and breadcrumbs, then chill for 20 minutes.

Heat the oil and butter in a frying pan, add the cutlets and brown on both sides. Lower the heat and cook for 6 minutes on each side. Drain on kitchen paper and arrange on a warmed serving dish; keep warm.

Add the herbs and sherry to the pan and boil rapidly for 2 minutes, until thickened. Stir in the cream, and salt and pepper to taste.

Spoon over the cutlets and serve immediately, garnished with the olives and sage.

Serves 4

Chicken Livers in Marsala

500 g (1 lb) chicken
  livers
25 g (1 oz) butter
2 onions, chopped
1 clove garlic, crushed
½ teaspoon chilli
  powder
125 g (4 oz) button
  mushrooms, sliced
150 ml (¼ pint)
  Marsala
1 teaspoon dried
  mixed herbs
dash of Worcester-
  shire sauce
salt and pepper
142 ml (5 fl oz)
  double cream
chopped thyme to
  garnish

Rinse the chicken livers thoroughly and pat dry with kitchen paper. Melt the butter in a pan, add the onions and garlic and fry until lightly browned. Stir in the chilli powder and chicken livers and cook for 5 minutes. Stir in the mushrooms and Marsala. Cook for 5 minutes, then add the herbs, Worcestershire sauce, and salt and pepper to taste. Add the cream, bring to the boil and cook for 2 minutes, stirring until thickened.

Garnish with thyme and serve with rice or pasta, and a green salad.
Serves 6

Chicken Breasts in Vermouth

1 tablespoon oil
1 clove garlic, thinly
  sliced
1 large onion, sliced
6 boneless chicken
  breasts, skinned
salt and pepper
150 ml (¼ pint) dry
  white vermouth
1 tablespoon each
  chopped tarragon
  and parsley
142 ml (5 fl oz)
  double cream
TO GARNISH:
lemon slices
tarragon leaves

Heat the oil in a pan, add the garlic and onion and fry until lightly browned; remove and set aside.

Season the chicken with salt and pepper to taste, add to the pan and brown on both sides. Return the onion and garlic to the pan, increase the heat and add the vermouth and herbs. Cook over high heat for 12 to 15 minutes, turning the chicken twice. Transfer the chicken to a warmed serving dish.

Pour the cream into the pan and cook over high heat, stirring, until the sauce has thickened. Spoon over the chicken and garnish with lemon slices and tarragon.

Serve immediately, with rice or creamed potatoes, if desired.
Serves 6

Chicken with Walnuts

4 spring onions
50 g (2 oz) walnuts
4 large boneless
    chicken breasts
1 small red pepper,
    cored and seeded
2 courgettes
50 g (2 oz) button
    mushrooms
2 tablespoons oil
2 cloves garlic, sliced
1 small piece root
    ginger, shredded
50 g (2 oz)
    mangetouts
2 tablespoons soy
    sauce
1 tablespoon dry
    sherry

Roughly chop the spring onions and walnuts. Thinly slice the chicken, red pepper and courgettes.

Heat the oil in a large frying pan or wok, add the garlic, ginger and spring onions and fry for 1 minute. Add the chicken and cook for 5 minutes, until browned on all sides. Add the remaining ingredients, increase the heat and cook, stirring constantly, for 3 minutes.

Turn into a warmed serving dish and serve immediately, with noodles or rice.

Serves 4

Creole-Style Prawns

1 tablespoon oil
1 large onion, chopped
1 clove garlic, crushed
2 celery sticks, thinly
 sliced
350 g (12 oz)
 tomatoes, skinned
1 green pepper, cored
 and seeded
salt and pepper
4 tablespoons dry
 white wine
1 tablespoon tomato
 purée
500 g (1 lb) peeled
 prawns
2 drops Tabasco sauce
1 teaspoon Worcester-
 shire sauce
1 tablespoon chopped
 parsley

Heat the oil in a pan, add the onion and garlic and fry until lightly browned. Add the celery and cook for 2 minutes.

Cut the tomatoes in half, remove the seeds and chop the flesh. Finely chop the green pepper. Add the tomatoes and pepper to the pan with salt and pepper to taste. Stir in the wine and tomato purée. Bring to the boil and simmer, uncovered, for 20 minutes.

Stir in the prawns, Tabasco and Worcestershire sauce. Simmer for 5 minutes, then stir in the parsley. Serve immediately, garnished with lemon twists and celery leaves, if liked. Serve with rice or pasta and a green salad.

Serves 6

Mediterranean Seafood

15 g (½ oz) butter
2 shallots, chopped
150 ml (¼ pint) dry
 white wine
2 tablespoons dry
 sherry
1 teaspoon French
 mustard
pinch of cayenne
dash of Worcester
 shire sauce
142 ml (5 fl oz)
 double cream
2 × 177 g (6 oz)
 cans crabmeat,
 drained
250 g (8 oz) peeled
 prawns
salt and pepper
2-3 tablespoons grated
 Parmesan cheese

Melt the butter in a pan, add the shallots and cook until softened, without browning. Pour in the wine and sherry, bring to the boil and boil rapidly until thickened and reduced by half.

Stir in the mustard, cayenne and Worcestershire sauce and cook for 2 minutes. Add the cream, bring to the boil, and boil for 5 to 7 minutes, stirring occasionally, until thickened.

Remove from the heat, stir in the fish and season with salt and pepper to taste.

Sprinkle with the cheese and serve immediately. Garnish with lime slices and herbs if liked, and serve rice or new potatoes and a tossed mixed salad as accompaniments.

Serves 4

LOW CALORIE DISHES

Hot Crab

15 g (½ oz) butter
1 onion, chopped
2 small cooked crabs,
  cleaned
juice of ½ lemon
dash of Worcester-
  shire sauce
salt and pepper
1 tablespoon fresh
  breadcrumbs
1 tablespoon grated
  Parmesan cheese
TO GARNISH:
parsley sprigs
4 lemon twists

Melt the butter in a pan, add the onion and cook for 5 to 7 minutes, without browning. Remove and cool.

Remove the crabmeat from each shell and flake; reserve the shells. Stir the lemon juice and Worcestershire sauce into the crabmeat with salt and pepper to taste. Stir in the onion and spoon into the shells. Sprinkle with the breadcrumbs and cheese.

Place on a baking sheet and cook in a preheated moderate oven, 180°C (350°F), Gas Mark 4, for 20 minutes, until heated through and golden brown.

Garnish with parsley and lemon twists and serve immediately.
Serves 2

Grilled Sole with Prawn Sauce

4 sole fillets
juice of 1 lemon
25 g (1 oz) butter or
   low-fat spread
SAUCE:
250 g (8 oz) peeled
   prawns
finely grated rind and
   juice of 1 lemon
1 tablespoon each
   chopped parsley
   and chives
salt and pepper
TO GARNISH:
few cooked whole
   prawns
lemon slices

Sprinkle the fish with the lemon juice, dot with the fat and cook under a preheated medium grill for 2 to 3 minutes on each side.

Meanwhile, prepare the sauce. Put the prawns, lemon rind and juice, herbs, and salt and pepper to taste in a pan and heat gently.

Roll up the sole fillets and arrange on serving plates. Spoon over the prawn sauce. Garnish with whole prawns and lemon slices and serve immediately.
Serves 4

Asparagus and Fish Salad

2 squid
24 mussels
150 ml (¼ pint) dry
  white wine
150 ml (¼ pint) fish
  stock
1 bouquet garni
salt and pepper
12 cooked whole
  prawns
250 g (8 oz) frozen
  asparagus
4 spring onions
2 celery sticks
50 g (2 oz) button
  mushrooms
DRESSING:
1 clove garlic, crushed
2 tablespoons natural
  yogurt
1 tablespoon lemon
  juice
1 tablespoon chopped
  parsley
dash of Tabasco sauce

Clean the squid and cut into rings. Place the mussels and squid in a pan and pour over the wine and stock. Add the bouquet garni and salt and pepper to taste. Bring to the boil and simmer for 4 to 5 minutes, until the mussels open; drain and discard any that have not opened; cool. Discard one side of each shell. Mix in the prawns.

Cook the asparagus in boiling salted water for 5 minutes or until just tender. Drain and cool under running cold water. Drain thoroughly and cut into 5 cm (2 inch) lengths. Chop the spring onions, and thinly slice the celery and mushrooms. Place in a salad bowl with the asparagus and mix well. Stir in the fish.

Mix the dressing ingredients together, seasoning well with salt and pepper, and spoon over the fish and asparagus. Serve immediately.
Serves 4 to 6

Gazpacho Salad

1 each green, red and
  yellow pepper
4 large tomatoes
1 small cucumber
1 Spanish onion
4 tablespoons
  chopped parsley
few black olives
DRESSING:
4 tablespoons olive oil
2 tablespoons wine
  vinegar
2 cloves garlic, crushed
pinch of ground cumin
1 teaspoon honey
2 spring onions,
  chopped
salt and pepper

Remove the core and seeds from the peppers and thinly slice them; roughly chop the tomatoes. Remove the seeds from the cucumber and chop. Finely chop the onion.

Layer the pepper, tomatoes, cucumber and onion in a glass bowl. Sprinkle the parsley liberally over each layer.

Mix all the dressing ingredients together, with salt and pepper to taste, and pour over the salad. Cover and leave to stand for 15 minutes before serving. Arrange the black olives on top to serve.
Serves 2 to 4
FOR NON-SLIMMERS: Serve with hot crusty garlic bread (see page 25).

Summer Grilled Trout

4 trout, cleaned
salt and pepper
1 tablespoon low-fat
    spread
4 spring onions,
    chopped
1 tablespoon chopped
    parsley
juice of ½ lemon
few dill sprigs
TO GARNISH:
dill sprigs
lemon wedges

Season the trout with salt and pepper
to taste. Mix together the low-fat
spread, spring onions, parsley,
lemon juice and dill. Divide the
mixture into 4 portions and put into
the cavities in the trout.

Cook under a preheated medium
grill for 5 to 7 minutes on each side,
until cooked.

Arrange on a warmed serving dish
and serve immediately, garnished
with dill and lemon wedges.
Serves 4

Parsley Chicken

8 tablespoons
  chopped parsley
2 tablespoons
  chopped chives
1 tablespoon chopped
  tarragon
2 shallots or 1 small
  onion, finely
  chopped
50 g (2 oz) button
  mushrooms, finely
  chopped
1/3 × 227 g (8 oz)
  tub skimmed milk
  soft cheese
salt and pepper
1 × 1.5 kg (3 lb)
  oven-ready chicken
1 clove garlic, thinly
  sliced
6 tablespoons dry
  white wine
parsley sprigs to
  garnish

Place 6 tablespoons of the parsley, the chives, tarragon, shallots or onion, and mushrooms in a bowl. Add the cheese, season well with salt and pepper and mix thoroughly until soft.

Season the chicken inside and out with salt and pepper.

Carefully lift the skin away from the breast and legs by sliding your fingers between the skin and flesh, taking care not to pierce the skin. Insert the parsley mixture, patting it to an even layer over the breast and thighs. Place in a roasting pan.

Cook in a preheated moderate oven, 180°C (350°F), Gas Mark 4, for 1½ to 1¾ hours, until tender. Transfer to a warmed serving dish.

Pour off the fat from the roasting pan. Add the garlic and wine and boil rapidly for 10 minutes until the liquid has thickened. Stir in the remaining parsley.

Spoon the sauce over the chicken to serve. Garnish with parsley sprigs.
Serves 4

Lambs' Liver with Thyme

1 tablespoon low-fat
  spread
1 onion, finely
  chopped
1 clove garlic, thinly
  sliced
500 g (1 lb) lambs'
  liver, thinly sliced
3 tablespoons
  chopped thyme
salt and pepper
juice of 1 lime or
  ½ lemon
TO GARNISH:
lime or lemon slices
thyme sprigs

Melt the low-fat spread in a pan, add the onion and garlic and cook for 5 minutes. Add the liver and brown quickly on both sides. Add the thyme and season well with salt and pepper. Sprinkle over the lime or lemon juice.

Transfer to a warmed serving dish, garnish with lime or lemon slices and thyme and serve immediately.
Serves 4

Tandoori Turkey Breasts

1 teaspoon chilli
  powder
1 small piece ginger
  root, very finely
  chopped
2 cloves garlic, crushed
1 teaspoon each
  ground coriander
  and cumin
2 teaspoons paprika
salt and pepper
300 g (10.4 oz)
  natural yogurt
1 tablespoon lemon
  juice
4 boneless turkey
  breasts
TO GARNISH:
shredded lettuce
onion rings
mint sprigs
lemon twists

Put the chilli powder, ginger, garlic, coriander, cumin and paprika in a large bowl, with salt and pepper to taste. Stir in the yogurt and lemon juice.

Place the turkey breasts in a shallow dish and spoon over the yogurt mixture. Cover and leave in the refrigerator overnight.

Remove the turkey from the marinade. Cook under a preheated moderate grill for 10 to 12 minutes on each side, basting frequently with the marinade, until the turkey is cooked through.

Arrange the lettuce on a plate, place the turkey on top and garnish with onion rings, mint sprigs and lemon twists. Serve immediately.

Serves 4

NOTE: If using small turkey breasts, serve two per person.

Coriander Lamb

2 cloves garlic, thinly sliced
½ teaspoon chilli powder
2 teaspoons ground ginger
1 teaspoon ground coriander
2 tablespoons chopped coriander leaves
150 g (5.2 oz) natural yogurt
salt and pepper
4 lamb chump chops
TO GARNISH:
lime or lemon wedges
coriander leaves

Put the garlic, chilli powder, ginger, ground coriander, coriander leaves and yogurt in a bowl, with salt and pepper to taste; mix well.

Place the chops in a shallow dish, spoon over the yogurt mixture, cover and leave to marinate for 2 hours, turning occasionally.

Remove from the marinade. Cook under a preheated moderately hot grill for 8 to 10 minutes on each side, until cooked through and browned, basting frequently with the marinade.

Serve hot, garnished with lime or lemon wedges and coriander.
Serves 4

Green Pepper Steak

2 × 150 g (5 oz)
    sirloin or fillet
    steaks
salt
2 tablespoons green
    peppercorns
1 tablespoon chopped
    thyme
1 clove garlic, crushed
50 g (2 oz) button
    mushrooms, sliced
120 ml (4 fl oz) dry
    red wine
dash of Worcester-
    shire sauce
1 teaspoon French
    mustard
2 spring onions,
    chopped
thyme sprigs to
    garnish

Season the steaks with salt. Press in the peppercorns and thyme.

Cook under a preheated hot grill for 2 to 3 minutes on each side, until browned, or until cooked according to taste.

Meanwhile, put the garlic, mushrooms and wine in a pan and bring to the boil. Boil rapidly until reduced and thickened, then stir in the Worcestershire sauce, mustard and spring onions.

Arrange the steaks on a warmed serving dish and spoon over the sauce. Garnish with thyme and serve immediately, with a green salad or vegetable.

Serves 2

Veal Scaloppine with Tomatoes

2 tablespoons oil
2 cloves garlic, thinly
   sliced
500 g (1 lb) veal
   escalope, very
   thinly sliced and
   pounded flat
salt and pepper
250 ml (8 fl oz) dry
   white wine
500 g (1 lb) tomatoes,
   skinned, seeded
   and chopped
dash of Worcester-
   shire sauce
1 tablespoon tomato
   purée
1 teaspoon each dried
   oregano and
   marjoram
dill sprigs to garnish
   (optional)

Heat the oil in a pan, add the garlic and cook for 1 minute. Season the veal with salt and pepper to taste, add to the pan and brown quickly on both sides.

Pour off any oil. Add the wine and tomatoes to the pan, bring to the boil and boil rapidly for 10 minutes, until the sauce has thickened. Stir in the Worcestershire sauce, tomato purée and herbs and cook for 5 minutes.

Transfer to a warmed serving dish and serve immediately, garnished with dill if liked.
Serves 4

INDEX